BALA
TO
LLANDUDNO

Vic Mitchell and Keith Smith

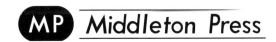

MP Middleton Press

Front cover: Pannier tank no. 7442 takes water at Trawsfynydd, having climbed over the mountains from Bala. Sadly no details are on record. (Colour-Rail.com)

Back cover upper: Green DMUs were introduced into the Conway Valley in 1956 and no. 101685 was repainted to form a heritage replica. It is seen at Blaenau Ffestiniog on 27th August 1994. (M.J.Stretton)

Back cover lower: A Hertfordshire Railtour arrived at Blaenau Ffestiniog on 18th April 1998 behind no. 59205 L. Keith McNair. *Alongside is FR Funkey Bo-Bo diesel* Vale of Ffestiniog, *in the same livery. (M.J.Stretton)*

Published November 2010

ISBN 978 1 906008 87 1

© Middleton Press, 2010

Design Deborah Esher

Published by
   Middleton Press
   Easebourne Lane
   Midhurst
   West Sussex
   GU29 9AZ
Tel: 01730 813169
Fax: 01730 812601
Email: info@middletonpress.co.uk
www.middletonpress.co.uk

Printed in the United Kingdom by Henry Ling Limited, at the Dorset Press, Dorchester, DT1 1HD

INDEX

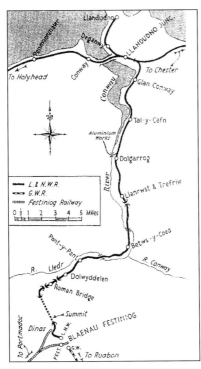

I. LNWR route as in 1920

II. GWR stations are shown as in 1935

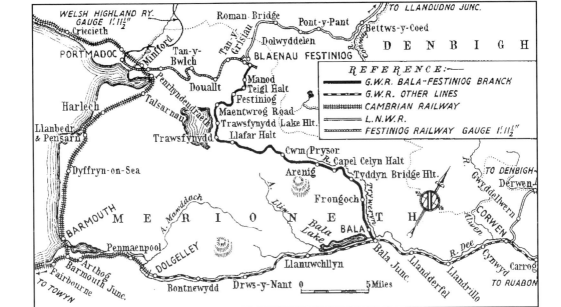

ACKNOWLEDGEMENTS

We are very grateful for the assistance received from many of those mentioned in the credits, also to B.Bennett, B.W.L.Brooksbank, A.R.Carder, C.Cartwright, G.Croughton, J.B.Horne, S.C.Jenkins, C.J.Keylock, E.Hancock, J.Langford, N.Langridge, B.Lewis, J.H.Meredith, Mr D. and Dr S.Salter, D.Smith, M.Turvey, T.Walsh, Dr J.Willis and especially our always supportive wives, Barbara Mitchell and Janet Smith.

GEOGRAPHICAL SETTING

Our journey starts in the upper Dee Valley where the south flowing Afon Tryweryn enters it, close to the terminal morain of Llyn Tegid (Bala Lake). The railway ran close to this river to the watershed at Llyn Tryweryn, but part of its valley was flooded after the line closed to form a two-mile long reservoir called Llyn Celyn.

The summit of the pass reaches 1315ft and the descent to Trawsfynydd was through infertile mountainous country, close to the Afon Prysor. This drains into another artificial lake, which was created to serve the 1928 Maentwrog Power Station. Its catchment area was extended southward in 1958, the year in which a nuclear power station was authorised. This also used lake water, but for cooling purposes. A new dam was built in 1988-92.

The remainder of the route to Blaenau Ffestinog is around 700ft above sea level and the final two miles is in the slate producing area. The town is surrounded on all but its south side by evidence of slate working and also the inclines linking the levels. Blaenau Tunnel passes through a two-mile long bore, deep under the southeast part of Snowdonia. Its northern portal is near the upper end of the Afon Lledr, which the route follows down to its confluence with the Afon Conwy, 1½ miles south of Betws-y-Coed. This growing water course is close to the railway for most of the remainder of the journey to the leisure resort of Llandudno.

Much of the rock is of volcanic origin and of a great age. In some areas it had been subjected to enormous pressure at high temperatures, while deep under the sea. Five rich and thick veins of slate have been worked in the Blaenau district as a result, but output has almost ceased. The lines between Bala and Blaenau inclusive were built in Merionethshire, but north of the latter they were in Carnarvonshire, except for three Denbighshire stations, noted later.

The maps are to the scale of 25ins to 1 mile, with north at the top unless otherwise indicated. Welsh spelling and hyphenation has varied over the years and so we have generally used the form of the period.

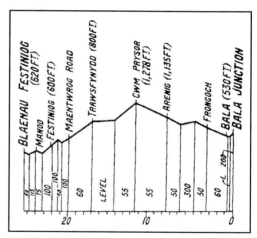

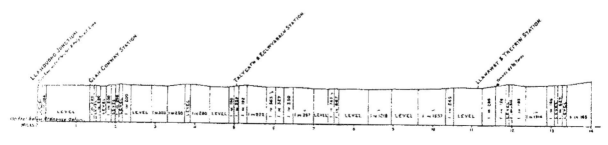

HISTORICAL BACKGROUND

The Festiniog Railway was the first line in the district and it carried slate from Blaenau Festiniog to the ships at Portmadoc from 1836. It was built to 1ft 11½ ins gauge, was steam worked from 1863 and carried passengers from 1865.

The first main line was that of the Chester & Holyhead Railway and it came into use between Chester and Bangor in 1848. A branch from it to Llandudno was opened by the St. George's Railway & Harbour Company on 1st October 1858. This became part of the London & North Western Railway in 1873 and the C&HR followed in 1879.

The Conway & Llanrwst Railway came into use on 17th June 1863 and was absorbed by the LNWR in 1867. It extended the branch to Bettws-y-Coed on 6th April 1868 and to Dinas on 22nd July 1879. The final ½ mile to Blaenau Festiniog followed on 1st April 1881.

In the meantime, narrow gauge trains had begun running south from this town to Festiniog itself on 30th May 1868. They were provided by the Festiniog & Blaenau Railway until 5th September 1883.

The Great Western Railway began operating between Ruabon and Dolgelley in 1868 on tracks built by local companies. The Bala & Festiniog Railway was opened between those places on 1st November 1882 and trains continued to Blaenau from 10th September 1883, the former narrow gauge line of the F&BR having been acquired and relaid. The GWR operated the route from those dates and owned it all from 1910.

The LNWR became part of the London Midland & Scottish Railway in 1923. With the advent of war in 1939, the passenger service on the FR was withdrawn, but it continued to carry some slate over most of its length until 1946. This traffic was retained on ¼ mile of its track in Blaenau Ffestiniog, preventing the two standard gauge termini being joined.

Upon nationalisation in 1948, the LMS lines in the area became part of the London Midland Region of British Railways, while the GWR formed the Western Region.

The route between Bala Town and Blaenau Ffestiniog Central was closed to passengers on 4th January 1960 and to goods on 28th January 1961, but the former station retained a service from the south until 18th January 1965.

The establishment of a nuclear power station north of Trawsfynydd necessitated provision of rail transport for its waste products. This was achieved by retaining the northern part of the closed branch and providing a link between the two terminal sites in Blaenau Ffestiniog. This opened on 20th April 1964; it did not impact on the FR, as its slate traffic had ceased and it did not reopen to that town until 1982. The complex alterations needed there are illustrated in the centre part of this album. Nuclear waste traffic ceased on 8th August 1995 (officially) and the line was mothballed.

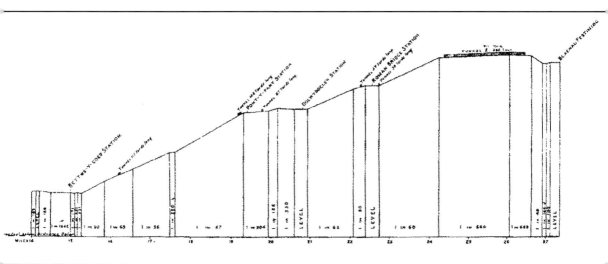

PASSENGER SERVICES

Festiniog & Blaenau Railway

The initial timetable offered six weekday trains with two extra on Saturdays. By 1878 there were four, still with the Saturday extras, a service which lasted to the end in 1883. There were no Sunday trains, but there were additional ones for quarrymen.

Bala Northwards

The first trains made connection with those of the F&BR at Festiniog and there were four on weekdays. The branch carried no Sunday trains.

By 1903 there were five, plus one starting at Trawsfynydd at 3.20pm. The same applied in 1923, but the evening trains ran on Thursdays and Saturdays only. The 1943 timetable had only three through trains, as did the final one, but this carried a late evening train on Saturdays.

Llandudno Southwards

The initial branch service ran between Llandudno and Conway, then the only other town in the district, reversal at the junction being necessary. This lasted for about a year. There were no Sunday trains on this short branch until 1904.

Following the opening to Bettws-y-Coed, six trains were provided, weekdays only. The frequency in sample years is on the right, with the Sunday figure in brackets.

There were a few additional short workings as far as Bettws-y-Coed, 3(4) being the figures as late as 1959. The Sunday trains often ran in the Summer only, terminating at Bettws-y-Coed in the steam era. Summer Sunday trains returned in 1975 and in 1989 they were extended over the new link to Maentwrog Road and on to Trawsfynydd siding for 1990 only.

1879-5	(0)
1903-7	(1)
1923-7	(0)
1934-12	(5)
1943-6	(0)
1955-10	(0)
1959-9	(0)
1979-8	(2)
2000-7	(3)

June 1869

October 1923

April 1943

LLANDUDNO AND BLAENAU FFESTINIOG—Weekdays only.

Miles	Station					SX	SO	SO	SO	SO	SO	SX		SX	SX	SO					SX	SO					ThO	SO	
			a.m.	a.m.	a.m.	a.m.	a.m.	p.m.	a.m.	a.m.	a.m.	p.m.	p.m.	p.m.	p.m.	p.m.	p.m.	p.m.	p.m.	p.m.	p.m.	p.m.	p.m.		p.m.	p.m.	p.m.	p.m.	p.m.
0	Llandudno	Z ...dep.	...	...	7 40	...	10 35	10 15	10 30	10 35	...	12 5	12 10	...	2 0	2 45	2 50	...	3 38	...	4 5	...	...	...	5 30	...	8 10	10 50	10 50	...
1¼	Deganwy	Z „	-	-	7 44	.	10 40	10 20	.	.	.	12 10	12 15	.	2 5	2 50	2 54	.	3 42	.	4 10	.	.	.	5 34	.	8 14	10 54	10 54	.
3	Llandudno Junction	arr.	...	...	7 49	...	10 45	10 25	10 39	10 45	...	12 15	12 20	...	2 10	2 55	2 59	...	3 47	...	4 15	...	...	...	5 39	...	8 19	10 59	10 59	...
		dep.	4 55	5 40	.	7 56	10 53	.	Runs 2nd July to 10th September inclusive.	Runs until 25th June inclusive also 17th September.	10 53	.	.	12 30	2 16	.	.	3 5	.	3 52	.	4 48	4 48	.	.	6 0	8 28	11 2	11 2	.
4¼	Glan Conway		...	...	...	8 0	10 57	...			10 57	...	...	12 34	2 20	...	...	3 9	...	3 56	...	4 52	4 52	...	...	6 4	8 32	...	...	...
8¼	Tal-y-Cafn & Eglwysbach		5 7	5 51	.	8g14	11 4	.			11 4	-	-	12 41	2 27	.	.	3 19	.	4 3	.	4 59	4 59	.	.	6 11	8 42	11 15	11 15	.
11¼	Dolgarrog		5⊦14	5⊦59	...	8 22	11 11	...			11 11	...	...	12 48	2 34	...	...	3 26	...	4 10	...	5 6	5 6	...	...	6 18	8 49	...	...	...
14¼	Llanrwst & Trefriw		5 25	6 8	.	8E33	11 20	.			11 20	.	.	12 56	2 42	.	.	3 34	.	4 18	.	5 17	5 17	.	.	6 28	8 57	11 29	11 29	.
18	Betws-y-Coed	arr.	5 33	6 16	...	8 41	11 28	...			11 28	...	...	1 4	2 50	...	...	3 42	...	4 26	...	5 25	5 25	...	...	6 36	9 5	11 37	11 37	...
		dep.	5 36	6 19	.	8 46	11 31	.			11 31	.	.	1 8	.	.	.	3 43	.	4 29	.	.	5 38	.	.	6 39	9 6	.	11 40	.
22½	Pont-y-Pant		A	6 31	...	8 58	11 43	...			11 43	...	...	1 20	...	...	...	3 55	...	4 41	...	...	5 50	...	...	6 51	9 18	...	...	...
24	Dolwyddelen		5 54	6 37	.	9 6	11 49	.			11 49	.	.	1k29	.	.	.	4 2	.	4k50	.	.	5k59	.	.	6 57	9 26	.	11 58	.
25¾	Roman Bridge		6⊦ 1	6 44	...	9 13	11 56	...			11 56	...	...	1 36	...	...	...	4 9	...	4 58	...	...	6 6	...	...	7 5	9 32	...	...	...
30¼	Blaenau Ffestiniog North	arr.	6 14	6 57	.	9 26	12 9	.			12 9	.	.	1 49	.	.	.	4 22	.	5 11	.	.	6 19	.	.	7 18	9 45	.	12 16	.

Miles	Station				SX	SO	SO	SO	SX		SO	SO	SO	SX		SO	SO			SX						SX	SO				
			a.m.		a.m.	a.m.	a.m.	a.m.	a.m.		a.m.	p.m.	p.m.	p.m.		p.m.	p.m.		p.m.	p.m.	p.m.		p.m.	p.m.		p.m.	p.m.	p.m.		p.m.	
0	Blaenau Ffestiniog North	dep.	7 5	...	8 45	8 45	Runs until 10th September inclusive.	...	10 54	...	10 54	Runs 25th June to 10th September inclusive.	...	12 27	...	12 27	...	...	2 18	...	4 30	...	5 39	...	...	...	6 36	7 40	...	10 15	...
4¼	Roman Bridge		7 18	.	8 58	8 58		.	11 7	.	11 7		.	12 40	.	12 40	.	.	2 31	.	4 43	.	5 52	.	.	.	6 49	7 53	-	10 28	.
6¼	Dolwyddelen		7 24	...	9 4	9 4		...	11 13	...	11 13		...	12 46	...	12 46	...	...	2 37	...	4 49	...	5 58	...	...	...	6 59	7 59	...	10 34	...
7¾	Pont-y-Pant		7 28	,	9 8	9 8		.	11 17	.	11 17		.	12 50	.	12 50	.	-	2 41	.	4 53	.	6 2	.	.	.	7 3	8 3	.	10 38	.
12¼	Betws-y-Coed	arr.	7 40	...	9 20	9 20		...	11 29	...	11 29		...	1 2	...	1 2	...	...	2 53	...	5 5	...	6 14	...	...	...	7 16	8 15	...	10 50	...
		dep.	7 44	.	9 22	9 22		.	11 33	.	11 33		.	1 6	.	1 6	.	.	2 56	4 9	5 9	.	6 17	.	.	7 10	7 19	8 18	.	10 54	.
16	Llanrwst & Trefriw		7 51	...	9 29	9 29		...	11 40	...	11 40		...	1 13	...	1 13	...	...	3 3	4 19	5 16	...	6k28	...	...	7 17	7 26	8 26	...	11 1	...
19	Dolgarrog		7 58	.	9 36	9 36		.	11 48	.	11 48		.	1 20	.	1 20	.	.	3 10	4 27	5 24	.	6 36	.	.	7 26	7 35	8 34	.	.	.
22	Tal-y-Cafn & Eglwysbach		8 9	...	9 44	9 44		...	11 56	...	11 56		...	1 28	...	1 28	...	...	3 18	4 35	5 32	...	6 44	...	...	7 34	7 43	8 43	...	11 15	...
25¼	Glan Conway		8 16	.	9 51	9 51		.	12 3	.	12 3		.	1 35	.	1 35	.	.	3 25	4 42	5 39	.	6 51	.	.	7 41	7 50	8 50	.	.	.
27¼	Llandudno Junction	arr.	8 21	...	9 56	9 56		...	12 8	...	12 8		...	1 40	...	1 40	...	...	3 30	4 47	5 44	...	6 56	...	...	7 47	7 56	8 55	...	11 25	...
		Z dep.	8 33	.	10 2	.	10 4	10 30	12 20	.	.	12 16	12 33	1 45	.	.	1 45	.	3 32	4 57	5 55	.	.	7 3	.	7 53	8 2	9 30	.	-	-
28½	Deganwy	Z „	8 40	...	10 9	...	10 9	10 35	12 25	...	...	12 23	12 39	1 49	...	...	1 49	...	3 37	5 2	6 0	...	...	7 8	...	7 58	8 7	9 35	...	...	...
30¼	Llandudno	Z ... arr.	8 45	.	10 14	.	10 14	10 40	12 30	.	.	12 29	12 44	1 54	.	.	1 54	.	3 42	5 7	6 5	.	.	7 13	.	8 3	8 12	9 40	.	.	-

⊦—Stops only to set down passengers.
A—Stops only to set down passengers on notice being given to the guard at Betws-y-Coed.
E—Arrives Llanrwst and Trefriw 8.30 a.m.

SO—Saturdays only. SX—Saturdays excepted.
ThO—Thursdays only.
g—Arrives six minutes earlier.
k—Arrives four minutes earlier.

Z—For other trains, Llandudno to Llandudno Junction, see Table 84.

June 1955

LLANDUDNO AND BLAENAU FFESTINIOG NORTH—Weekdays only

Miles	Station																	SO						SX	SO			
			a.m.	a.m.		a.m.	a.m.		a.m.		p.m.		p.m.	p.m.	p.m.	p.m.	p.m.	p.m.	p.m.		p.m.	p.m.		p.m.	p.m.		p.m.	
0	LLANDUDNO	Z ... dep	...	...	...	7 32	7 40	...	10 35	...	12 10	...	2 10	2 45	...	3 38	...	4 5	...	5 30	...	...	6 20	...	...	6 55	...	8 15	...
1½	Deganwy	Z ... „	.	.	.	7 37	7 45	.	10 40	.	12 16	.	2 15	2 50	.	3 43	.	4 10	.	5 35	.	.	6 26	.	.	7 0	.	8 20	.
3	LLANDUDNO JUNCTION	Z ... arr	...	...	...	7 42	7 50	...	10 45	...	12 28	...	2 20	2 55	...	3 48	...	4 15	...	5 40	...	...	6 30	...	...	7 5	...	8 25	...
	„	Z ... dep	4 53	5 40	.	7 55	.	.	10 53	.	12 32	.	2 25	.	3 5	.	3 52	.	4 42	.	.	6 0	.	.	7 10	7 10	.	8 28	.
4¼	Glan Conway		...	...	...	8 1	...	...	10 57	...	12 36	...	2 29	...	3 9	...	3 56	...	4 46	...	...	6 4	...	...	7 14	7 14	...	8 32	...
8¼	Tal-y-Cafn & Eglwysbach		5 5	5 50	.	8 11	.	.	11 4	.	12 43	.	2 36	.	3 19	.	4 3	.	4 53	.	.	6 11	.	.	7 21	7 21	.	8 42	.
11¼	Dolgarrog		5⊦11	5⊦56	...	8 17	...	...	11 10	...	12 49	...	2 42	...	3 25	...	4 9	...	4 59	...	...	6 17	...	...	7 27	7 27	...	8 48	...
14¼	Llanrwst & Trefriw		5 19	6 3	.	8 25	.	.	11 16	.	12 56	.	2 49	.	3 31	.	4 16	.	5 8	.	.	6 24	.	.	7 33	7 33	.	8 54	.
18	Betws-y-Coed	arr	5 26	6 10	...	8 32	...	...	11 23	...	1 3	...	2 56	...	3 38	...	4 23	...	5 15	...	...	6 31	...	...	7 40	7 40	...	9 1	...
	„	dep	5 29	6 12	.	8 35	.	.	11 24	.	1 5	.	.	.	3 40	.	4 26	.	.	.	.	6 33	.	.	.	.	.	9 3	.
22¼	Pont-y-Pant		A	A	...	8 47	...	...	11 36	...	1 17	...	...	...	3 52	...	4 38	...	...	...	...	6 45	...	...	...	...	...	9 15	...
24	Dolwyddelen		5 46	6 29	.	8D57	.	.	11 42	.	1 22	.	.	.	3 57	.	4 45	.	.	.	.	6 50	.	.	.	.	.	9 20	.
25¾	Roman Bridge		5⊦53	6 36	...	9 4	...	...	11 49	...	1 29	...	...	...	4 4	...	4 52	...	...	...	...	6 57	...	...	...	...	...	9 27	...
30¼	BLAENAU FFESTINIOG NORTH	... arr	6 4	6 47	.	9 15	.	.	12 0	.	1 40	.	.	.	4 15	.	5 3	.	.	.	.	7 8	.	.	.	.	.	9 38	.

Miles	Station										SO		SX	SX	SX	SO			SO							SX		SO
			a.m.	a.m.	a.m.	p.m.		p.m.	p.m.		p.m.	p.m.	p.m.	p.m.	p.m.	p.m.	p.m.		p.m.	p.m.	p.m.	p.m.	p.m.	p.m.		p.m.		p.m.
0	BLAENAU FFESTINIOG NORTH	... dep	7 15	8 40	11 20	12 30	...	2 27	...	...	...	...	... TC—Betws-y-Coed to Rhyl arr. 6.9 p.m.	...	4 25	4 28	...	...	...	5 42	...	...	...	7 50	...	10 20	...	10 28
4¼	Roman Bridge		7 26	8 51	11 31	12 41	.	2 38	.	.	.	.	.	.	4 36	4 34	.	.	.	5 53	.	.	.	8 1	.	10 31	.	10 31
6¼	Dolwyddelen		7 32	8 56	11 40	12 47	...	2 44	...	...	...	...	...	...	4 42	4 42	...	...	...	5 59	...	...	...	8 7	...	10 38	...	10 38
7¾	Pont-y-Pant		7 36	9 2	11 44	12 51	.	2 48	.	.	.	.	.	.	4 46	4 46	.	.	.	6 3	.	.	.	8 11	.	10 42	.	10 42
12¼	Betws-y-Coed	arr	7 47	9 13	11 55	1 2	...	2 59	...	...	...	...	...	...	4 57	4 57	...	...	...	6 14	...	...	...	8 22	...	...	...	...
	„	dep	7 49	9 14	11 56	1 4	.	3 0	.	.	3 43	.	4 6	.	4 58	4 58	.	.	5 34	6 15	.	7 45	.	8 23	.	10 53	.	10 53
16	Llanrwst & Trefriw		7 55	9 20	12 2	1 10	...	3 6	...	...	3 49	...	4E17	...	5 4	5F 7	...	...	6 0	6 24	...	7 51	...	8 29	...	10 59	...	11 2
19	Dolgarrog		8 1	9 26	12 8	1 16	.	3 12	.	.	3 55	.	4 23	.	5 10	5 13	.	.	.	6 30	.	7 57	.	8 35	.	.	.	.
22	Tal-y-Cafn & Eglwysbach		8 9	9 32	12 14	1 22	...	3 18	...	...	4 4	...	4 29	...	5 16	5 19	...	...	6 13	6 36	...	8 3	...	8 41	...	11 10	...	11 13
25¾	Glan Conway		8 15	9 38	12 20	1 28	.	3 24	.	.	4 10	.	4 35	.	5 22	5 25	.	.	.	6 42	.	8 9	.	8 48	.	.	.	11 20
27¼	LLANDUDNO JUNCTION	Z ... arr	8 21	9 44	12 26	1 34	...	3 30	...	...	4 17	...	4 41	...	5 28	5 31	...	...	6 23	6 48	...	8 15	...	8 53	...	11 21	...	11 28
	„	Z ... dep	8 33	9 50	12 29	1 37	.	.	3 33	.	.	4 40	.	4 57	5 30	.	5 53	.	6 30	.	7 3	.	8 23	9 5	.	.	.	.
28½	Deganwy	Z	8 39	9 54	12 33	1 41	...	...	3 36	...	...	4 45	...	5 1	5 34	...	5 59	...	6 34	...	7 8	...	8 27	9 9	...	...	...	...
30¼	LLANDUDNO	Z ... arr	8 44	10 0	12 39	1 47	.	.	3 41	.	.	4 50	.	5 7	5 40	.	6 4	.	6 40	.	7 13	.	8 32	9 15	.	.	.	.

⊦—Stops only to set down passengers.
A—Calls to set down only on notice being given to the Guard at Betws-y-Coed.
D—Arrives Dolwyddelen 8.51 a.m.

E—Arrives Llanrwst & Trefriw 4.12 p.m.
F—Arrives Llanrwst & Trefriw 5.4 p.m.
SO—Saturdays only.
SX—Saturdays excepted.

June 1958

September 1959

BALA and BLAENAU FFESTINIOG
WEEK DAYS ONLY

Mls		am		am		E	pm	S	
—	**Bala** dep	6 55	..	1155	..	3 40	5 35	8 55	..
2½	Frongoch	7 1	....	12 0	....	3 45	5 40	9 0	....
4¼	Tyddyn Bridge Halt	7 6	..	12 5	..	3 50	5 45	9 5	..
6	Capel Celyn Halt	7 13	....	1212	....	3 55	5 52	9 12	....
7¾	Arenig	7 19	..	1218	..	4 0	5 58	9 18	..
10½	Cwm Prysor Halt	7 26	....	1225	....	4 7	6 6	9 26	....
13¾	Bryncelynog Halt	7 35	..	1234	..	4 15	6 15	9 34	..
15	Llafar Halt	7 38	....	1238	....	4 18	6 19	9 39	....
16½	Trawsfynydd	8u 0	..	1245	..	4 25	6 24	9 45	..
18¼	Trawsfynydd Lake Halt	8 5	....	1250	....	....	6 29	9 50	....
19½	Maentwrog Road	8 8	..	1253	..	..	6 32	9 53	..
21½	**Festiniog**	8 15	....	1 0	....	....	6 39	9 59	....
22¼	Teigl Halt	8 19	..	1 4	..	..	6 43	10 4	..
23½	Manod Halt	8 25	....	1 10	....	....	6 50	10 9	....
24¾	**Blaenau Ffestiniog Cen. C.** arr	8 31	..	1 17	..	..	6 56	1015	..

	am		S		pm		S	E		pm	S	
Blaenau Ffestiniog Central dep	7 10	..	11 50	..	2 20	..	4 15	4 25	.	7 15	1025	..
Manod Halt	7 15	....	11 55	....	2 25	....	4 20	4 29	...	7 19	1030	...
Teigl Halt	7 21	..	12 0	..	2 30	..	4 25	4 34	.	7 25	1036	..
Festiniog	7 26	....	12 5	....	2 35	....	4 30	4 39	...	7 30	1040	...
Maentwrog Road	7 32	..	12 10	..	2 41	..	4 36	4 45	.	7 36	1046	..
Trawsfynydd Lake Halt	7 35	....	12 14	....	2 44	....	4 39	4 48	...	7 39	1049	....
Trawsfynydd	7 41	..	12t45	..	2 50	..	4 47	4 53	.	7 45	1055	..
Llafar Halt	7 46	....	12 50	....	2 55	....	4 52	....	...	7 50	....	....
Bryncelynog Halt	7 50	..	12 54	..	2 59	..	4 56	..	.	7 54	..	..
Cwm Prysor Halt	8 1	....	1 3	....	3 10	....	5 5	....	...	8 5	....	....
Arenig	8 7	..	1 9	..	3 16	..	5 13	5 14	.	8 11	..	..
Capel Celyn Halt	8 12	....	1 14	....	3 21	....	5 18	5 19	...	8 16	....	....
Tyddyn Bridge Halt	8 17	..	1 19	..	3 26	..	5 23	5 24	.	8 21	..	..
Frongoch	8 22	....	1 24	....	3 31	....	5 28	5 29	...	8 26	....	....
Bala arr	8 28	..	1 28	..	3 37	..	5 34	5 34	.	8 31	..	..

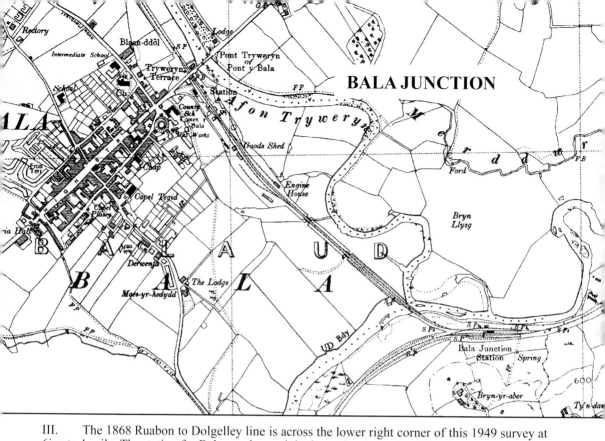

BALA JUNCTION

III.   The 1868 Ruabon to Dolgelley line is across the lower right corner of this 1949 survey at 6ins to 1 mile. The station for Bala was beyond the lower border until 1882. The population was 1544 in 1901 and 1640 in 1961.

1.   Seen from the island platform on 15th August 1953 is the 9.15am from Blaenau Ffestiniog, with 0-4-2T no. 5810 running round on the loop. The passengers sheltering from the rain are waiting for the train to Ruabon. The only other access to the station was across a field. (H.C.Casserley)

2.   The passenger line to and from Bala is on the left, the one in the foreground being a parallel goods line. Beyond the water tank is the signal box, which had 53 levers, seven of which were out of use. (R.K.Blencowe)

Other photographs of this junction can be seen in our
***Ruabon to Barmouth* album.**

3.   This photograph from 28th November 1964 has an empty train leaving the goods line, bound for the "Back Road" at the branch platform. Trains for the west could use this platform or the one in the foreground. The up platform was not bidirectional. (A.M.Davies)

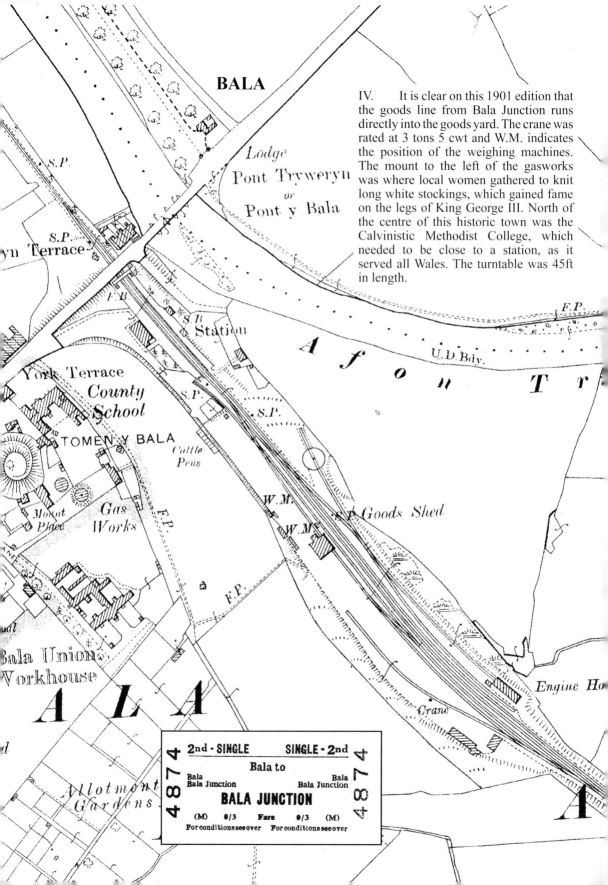

BALA

Lodge

Pont Tryweryn

or

Pont y Bala

IV.   It is clear on this 1901 edition that the goods line from Bala Junction runs directly into the goods yard. The crane was rated at 3 tons 5 cwt and W.M. indicates the position of the weighing machines. The mount to the left of the gasworks was where local women gathered to knit long white stockings, which gained fame on the legs of King George III. North of the centre of this historic town was the Calvinistic Methodist College, which needed to be close to a station, as it served all Wales. The turntable was 45ft in length.

S.P.

yn Terrace

S.P.

F.B.

S.B.

Station

A f o n   T r

U.D. Bdy.

F.P.

F.P.

York Terrace

County School

S.P.

S.P.

TOMEN Y BALA

Cattle Pens

Mount Place

Gas Works

F.P.

W.M.

W.M.

S.P. *Goods Shed*

Bala Union Workhouse

F.P.

F.P.

A L A

Crane

Engine Ho

Allotment Gardens

A

2nd - SINGLE	SINGLE - 2nd

4874   4874

Bala to

Bala
Bala Junction

Bala
Bala Junction

BALA JUNCTION

(M)   0/3   Fare   0/3   (M)

For conditions see over   For conditions see over

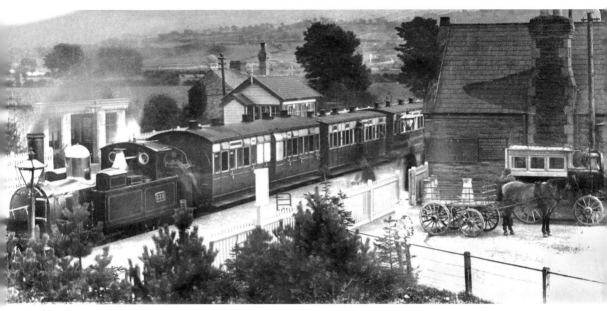

4.   Few postcards featured this station, but this one included goods and passenger road transport in about 1900, plus the impressive up waiting shelter. The class 517 0-4-2T is no. 539. The signal box was partially boarded in 1923 to form a staff room. There were 20 men here that year and 24 for most of the 1930s. (Lens of Sutton coll.)

5.   Both weigh offices are included in this record of 0-6-0T no. 5740 shunting on 15th August 1953. Few stations had a castellated goods shed. The ornamentation was to pacify a local objector and landowner. (H.C.Casserley)

6.	The main entrance was on the town side and fancy stonework was not demanded here. A shuttle service was worked to Bala Junction and 0-6-0PT no. 7443 is working it on 4th April 1959. (G.Adams/M.J.Stretton coll.)

7.	The route indicator on the right authorises the driver onto Down Siding. The 7300 class 2-6-0s seldom ran west of here, but could go to Trawsfynydd under restrictions. The goods yard closed on 2nd November 1964 and the site was cleared. The lamp room is on the left. The 1923 signal box had 26 levers and closed on 18th January 1965. The cattle dock siding is on the right. (G.Adams/M.J.Stretton coll.)

8.   No. 4617 has run in with the 2.20pm from Blaenau Ffestiniog and the guard has taken a quick route to the station, sometime in 1960. Items not seen so far are the road bridge, the water tank, the footbridge, the dull replacement for the Grecian waiting room and the adapted signal box. (D.A.Johnson coll.)

9.   A water tank surmounts the entrance to the engine shed and the coal stage was separate, on the adjacent siding. Closure date was 18th January 1965 and it was coded sub to 84J. There were seven crews based here at that time. (R.S.Carpenter)

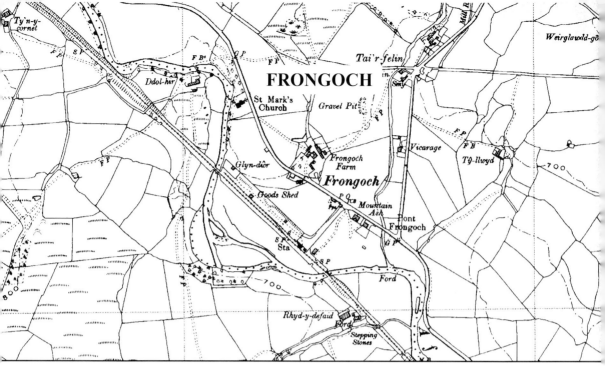

V.   The 1949 edition at 6ins to 1 mile shows the station to be within the meanders of the Afon Tryweryn. The road close to the railway was then the B4391, which wandered across moors to Ffestiniog.

10.   It is August 1956 and the crew of 0-6-0PT no. 7443 wait for the photographer and we spot the goods shed in the distance. The signal box was a block post, but no passing was possible. It had 11 levers. (A.M.Davies)

11.   The picking-up post for the token is in the foreground, along with its oil lamp. The platform lamps at the next halt were cared for by Frongoch staff. No. 9793 is working the 2.20pm from Blaenau Ffestiniog on a sunlit day in August 1958. (J.W.T.House/C.L.Caddy coll.)

VI.   The 1901 edition includes a rare distillery - Wales was not like Scotland. The house top left was for the station master. The goods yard closed on 28th January 1961. Between 1913 and 1938, there were two or sometimes three employees here.

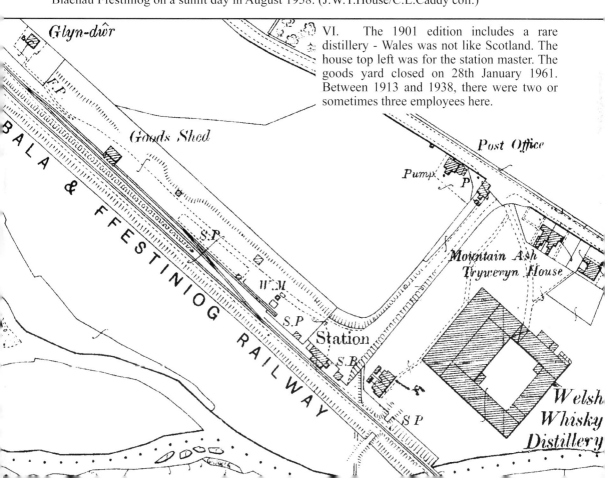

TYDDYN BRIDGE HALT

12.   The platform is in the distance in this view towards Bala on 21st January 1961. It came into use on 30th December 1930 and was largely for the benefit of walkers. The bridge had three spans and also carried the footpath. (S.C.L.Phillips/D.K.Jones coll.)

CAPEL CELYN HALT

13.   Both dates in caption 12 also apply here. The two lamps were cared for by Arenig staff. The west end of the reservoir is now in this vicinity. (S.C.L.Phillips/D.K.Jones coll.)

ARENIG

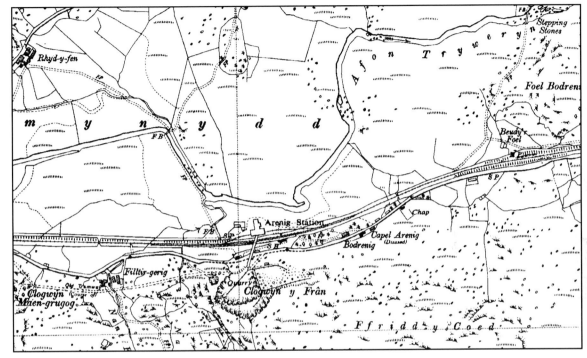

VII.   The 1949 edition of the 6ins to 1 mile map shows footpaths crossing marshland to reach the limited habitation. The quarry south of the line was that of the Arenig Granite Company, which started in 1908.

14.   The gates are for the private siding for loading granite. The quarry is on the left and the bridge supported a conveyor belt for the stone. All three photographs are from January 1961. (A.M.Davies)

15. Loaded granite wagons are on the left as 0-6-0PT no. 8727 passes through with cement wagons nearest to it. The contents were for use in the construction of the Tanygrisiau pumped storage scheme, which impinged on the FR west of Ffestiniog. (A.M.Davies)

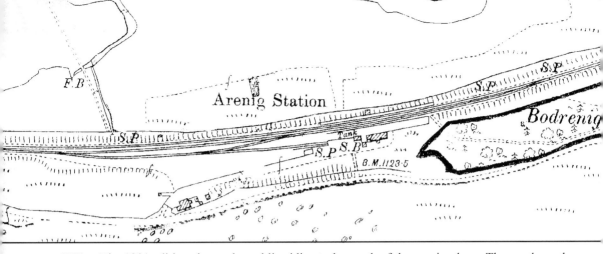

VIII.   The 1901 edition shows the public siding to be south of the passing loop. The goods yard has its own loop and closed on 28th January 1961. There was a staff of four in the 1930s.

16.   The last train was photographed from the crushing plant on 22nd January 1961. Much point rodding is evident, the signal box being on the right with a rodding tunnel under the tracks. The box had 25 levers. (WHR Heritage Group)

CWM PRYSOR HALT

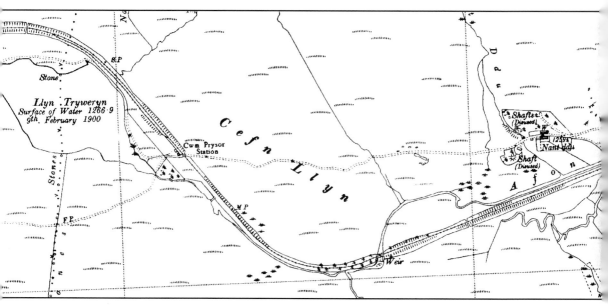

IX.   Opened on 1st September 1902, the station became a halt on 8th June 1953. A long loop is shown northwest of it, but there is little habitation. The loop was added in 1908 for troop trains.

17.   At around 1300ft above sea level, the route across the watershed could suffer extreme weather conditions, as experienced in February 1947. Apart from the obvious problem, the telephone wires would break. A pilotman would save the day. The signal box was in use only when required from 1945 to 1951, when it closed and the loop became a siding. The signals were then removed. (C.L.Caddy coll.)

18. The level crossing is behind the 3.40pm Bala to Trawsfynydd on 27th June 1956. No. 7443 has reached the summit after climbing at 1 in 55 for over two miles. It will now have a similar descent. There was a station mistress in charge here as early as 1912. (W.A.Camwell/SLS coll.)

19. The nine-arch viaduct was built on a curve which justified a check rail. New walls and railings were provided in 1953 and this photograph of empty cement wagons was taken in 1960. The structure remains standing as a memorial to the branch. (K.Robinson coll.)

LLAFAR HALT

20. This stop came into use on 1st March 1932 and was graced with a Pagoda shelter instead of a garden shed. It had settled down the hill somewhat by March 1959. (R.M.Casserley)

➜ X. The 1957 revision at 1ins to 1 mile has three stops marked at the bottom, the centre one being Llafar Halt. To the right of it is Bryncelynog Halt, which was of similar construction; it opened on 13th March 1939. The stop north of Trawsfynydd is Trawsfynydd Lake Halt and north of that is Maentwrog Road, the village being beyond the left border and over 500ft lower. The convoluted journey north is followed by three stations in close proximity and then the long straight tunnel, all described later.

October 1923

BALA and BLAENAU FESTINIOG.—Great Western.

Miles	Down.	mrn	mrn	mrn	mrn	E S aft	aft	E aft	aft	T aft				
	Bala........................dep.	6 55	...	9 20	1128	1140	...	3 45	5 40	8 40	...	...		
2¼	Frongoch................	7 1	...	9 26	1134	1149	...	3 55	5 46	8 46	...	...		
7¼	Arenig....................	7 18	...	9 38	1147	12 0	...	4 15	5 58	8 58	...	...		
10½	Cwm Prysor............	⋀	...	⋀	⋀	⋀	...	...	⋀	⋀	...	...		
16½	Trawsfynydd............	7 40	8 10	9 58	12 6	1220	3 20	...	5 19	9 17	...	...		
19½	Maentwrog Road......		8 18	10 6	1214	1228	3 30	...	6 27	9 25	...	...		
21½	Festiniog................		8 25	1013	1220	1234	3 40	...	6 34	9 33	...	...		
23½	Manod ......{401, 949}		8 35	1025	1227	1245	3 50	...	6 45	9 43	...	...		
24½	Blaenau Festiniog⸨ar.		8 41	1031	1234	1252	3 55	...	6 52	9 48	...	...		

Miles	Up.	mrn	mrn	S aft	S aft	aft 3 cl.	aft	E aft	E A S aft	aft			
	Blaenau Festiniog.....dep.	7 40	9 30	1220	...	2 35	4 25	...	5 45	7 10	...	...	
1½	Manod	7 47	9 37	1227	...	2 42	4 31	...	5 51	7 16	...	...	
3½	Festiniog................	7 57	9 47	1240	...	2 55	4 40	...	6 17	7 25	...	...	
5½	Maentwrog Road......	8 2	9 52	1247	...	3 0	4 46	...	6 6	7 30	...	...	
8½	Trawsfynydd............	8 9	9 59	1257	...	3 5	4 52	...	5 25	6 25	7 35	...	
14½	Cwm Prysor............	⋀	⋀	...	⋀	⋀	...	⋀	⋀	⋀	...	...	
17	Arenig....................	8 28	1018	...	1235	3 25	...	5 5	6 0	6 55	7 55	...	
22½	Frongoch	8 40	1030	...	1247	3 38	...	5 20	6 16	7 12	8	...	
24½	Bala 145 & above... arr.	8 45	1035	...	1252	3 43	...	5 37	6 32	7 27	8 13	...	

⋀ Stop when required; passengers wishing to alight must notify the Guard at either Arenig or Trawsfynydd.   A Thursdays only.
E Except Saturdays.   S Saturdays only.   T Thursdays and Saturdays.
⸨ ¼ mile to L. M. & S. Station and adjoining Welsh Highland and Festiniog Company's Station.

TRAWSFYNYDD

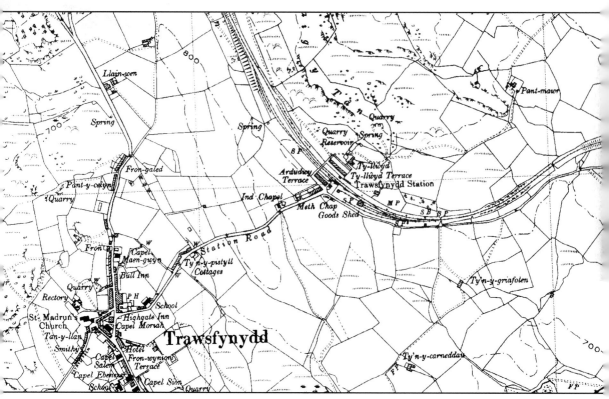

XI.   The 1949 survey at 6ins to 1 mile shows that the railway is close to the 800ft contour line. There was a population of 1595 in 1901 and 1878 in 1961. Above the station are the sidings for the Army camp, which were laid down in 1911. The A470 now bisects Station Road.

21.   This panorama of the down platform was taken soon after the second signal box was completed in 1911. The freight train may be working between the goods yard (left of the camera) and the Camp station, which is beyond the bridge. (Lens of Sutton coll.)

22.   A mixed train bound for Bala pauses, sometime in the 1950s. The line on the left served the cattle dock. All the buildings have been demolished. (W.A.Camwell/SLS coll.)

XII.   The 1901 survey shows the cottages for workers which surround the station. It even details the privies at the end of each garden.

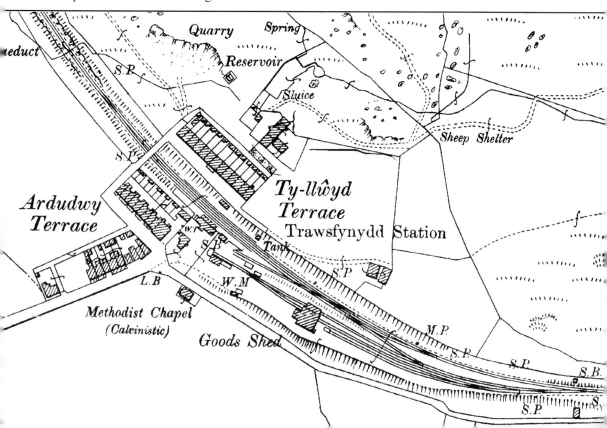

23.	A 1955 picture includes the lean-to, which served as an engine shed for one locomotive. The retired postal van gave more room for parcels. During the 1930s, there was a staff of five. (P.J.Garland/R.S.Carpenter coll.)

24.	The shed was occupied by 0-6-0PT no. 4683 on 11th September 1960. The goods shed contained a one-ton crane; the others are mobile. Freight traffic was not conveyed after 28th January 1961. (R.S.Carpenter)

TRAWSFYNYDD CAMP

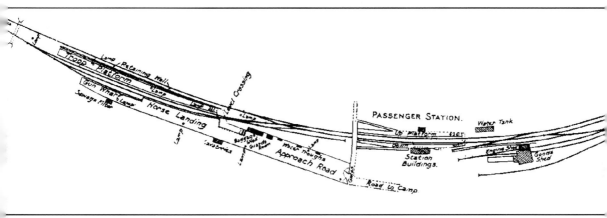

XIII.   The GWR track plan of 1912 shows the provision made for the Army to access its gunnery ranges on the moors. The camp opened in 1908, but it was a three-mile march from the station, uphill. The original station was soon overwhelmed and a timber platform was added. Work was completed on this special station in late 1911.

25.   This northward panorama is from about 1912 and includes two 0-6-0STs followed by a six-wheeled coach, bogie clerestory coaches, flat wagons for guns and finally a string of horse boxes. The running line is behind the fence, which was intended to prevent the horses being frightened by passing trains. (Lens of Sutton coll.)

26. The camp was very busy during both World Wars and was used into the 1950s. This view is from July 1964, more than three years after the last train movement. The route remained operational south to the goods yard, in case it was reopened for freight or military traffic. (C.L.Caddy)

TRAWSFYNYDD LAKE HALT

27. This stop came into use on 14th April 1934, apparently with fishermen in mind. It is seen in use by locals on 15th August 1953. (H.C.Casserley)

28.   Freight traffic over the entire branch ceased on 28th January 1961, but the line north of here was retained and was reopened on 20th April 1964 for nuclear flask traffic to Sellafield. The massive gantry made the transfer to and from road vehicles, which moved the flasks about ½ mile only. There was no loop here, just a short siding. (P.G.Hindley)

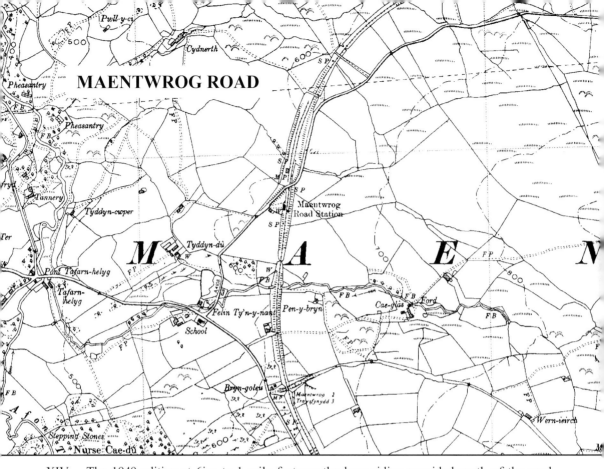

MAENTWROG ROAD

XIV. The 1949 edition at 6ins to 1 mile features the long siding provided north of the road bridge. Two were provided, but such detail is not always recorded at this scale. The tannery (left) despatched much leather by rail in the 1920s.

29. We can see the sidings as 0-6-0PT no. 7443 arrives with the 11.15am Blaenau Ffestiniog to Trawsfynydd on 27th June 1956. The sign refers to a 3-mile walk; Maentwrog was almost as far. The main building survives, in use as a dwelling. (W.A.Camwell/SLS coll.)

30.   The extent of the goods yard becomes evident in this 1957 view. The shed contained a one-ton crane and the yard closed on 28th January 1961 for public traffic. There was an 11-lever ground frame. Two men sufficed here in the 1930s. (M.Lloyd)

31.   Explosives were made at Cookes' factory at Penrhyndeudraeth and were mostly conveyed on the Cambrian Coast line. However, with the sudden closure of Barmouth Bridge to locomotives in April 1980, the dangerous products were loaded here. No. 47193 is in attendance on 16th June 1987 with one van and two barrier wagons. The traffic ceased on 22nd July 1988, after the factory caught fire. (L.Goddard)

32. The "Trawsfynydd Trekker" was one of a small number of special trains to venture south of the 1964 link. No. 31190 is leading with no. 31327 at the back on 27th August 1994 and they are passing the siding seen in the previous picture. A wooden platform had been built over it for Sunday trains in 1989. The last train to it ran on 10th September of that year.
(K.Robinson)

33. Nos 31130 and 31319 are seen on 19th May 1995 hauling nuclear waste from Trawsfynydd Power Station, which is evident in the background. Flooding near Llanrwst had closed the line for six days prior to this.
(L.Goddard)

FESTINIOG

XV.   The 1949 map at 6ins to 1 mile emphasises the curvature of the branch, notably over the three-arch Bryn Rodyn Viaduct (lower right) and near Teigl Halt (top right). The old village, together with Blaenau, recorded a population of 11,435 in 1901 and 6660 in 1961, following the collapse of the slate industry. On the left is a hairpin bend on the road from the valley. The local slate quarries were small and mostly east of the railway.

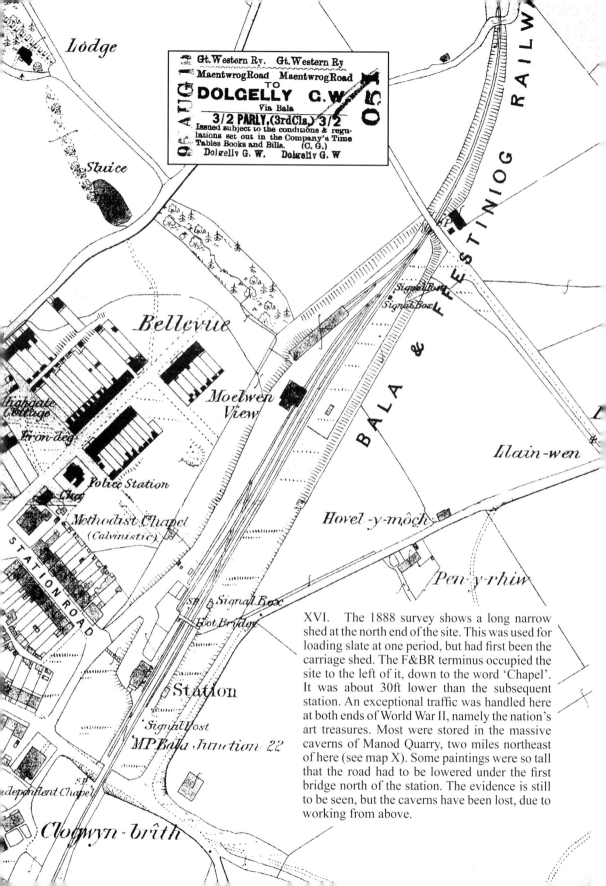

Lodge

Sluice

Bellevue

Moelwen View

Llain-wen

Highgate Cottage

Fron-deg

Police Station

Hovel-y-môch

Methodist Chapel (Calvinistic)

Pen-y-rhiw

STATION ROAD

SP   Signal Box

Foot Bridge

Station

Signal Post

MP Bala Junction 22

Independent Chapel

Clogwyn-brith

XVI.   The 1888 survey shows a long narrow shed at the north end of the site. This was used for loading slate at one period, but had first been the carriage shed. The F&BR terminus occupied the site to the left of it, down to the word 'Chapel'. It was about 30ft lower than the subsequent station. An exceptional traffic was handled here at both ends of World War II, namely the nation's art treasures. Most were stored in the massive caverns of Manod Quarry, two miles northeast of here (see map X). Some paintings were so tall that the road had to be lowered under the first bridge north of the station. The evidence is still to be seen, but the caverns have been lost, due to working from above.

34.　　　The goods shed is near the words Moelwyn View on the 1888 map and we look at its north end in the 1930s. In the foreground are rows of slates awaiting despatch and on the right is the former terminal site. There were three men here in 1913-38. (K.Robinson coll.)

35.　　　In the background is the mass of Manod Mawr, which rises to over 2000 ft and has Manod Quarry on the right. We have no details of the train bound for Bala from the deserted platform. The signal box had 20 levers and the right signal post was of concrete. The box closed with the goods yard on 28th January 1961. (W.A.Camwell/SLS coll.)

36.   Freight trains pass in the 1950s, with no. 9610 destined for Bala. This is the view from the signal box of the unusual double gable canopy, devoid of stanchions. (Dr G.B.Sutton)

37.   This photograph from 12th July 1964 shows that the up line through the station was retained for nuclear flask traffic, it having reopened three months earlier. No signalling was needed by that time. There is now no trace of the buildings. (C.L.Caddy)

TEIGL HALT

38.   We are approaching the stop on the 11.55am from Bala on 13th November 1952, hauled by 0-6-0PT no. 7447. The train has dropped at 1 in 100 onto the bridge and is now climbing at 1 in 75. The hut contained a telephone for use by men working on the line. (H.Ballantyne)

39.   We look in the other direction from the platform as 0-6-0PT no. 7431 approaches in January 1957. The bridge is over the ravine carrying the Afon Teigl and beyond it can be seen the change of gradient. (A.M.Davies coll.)

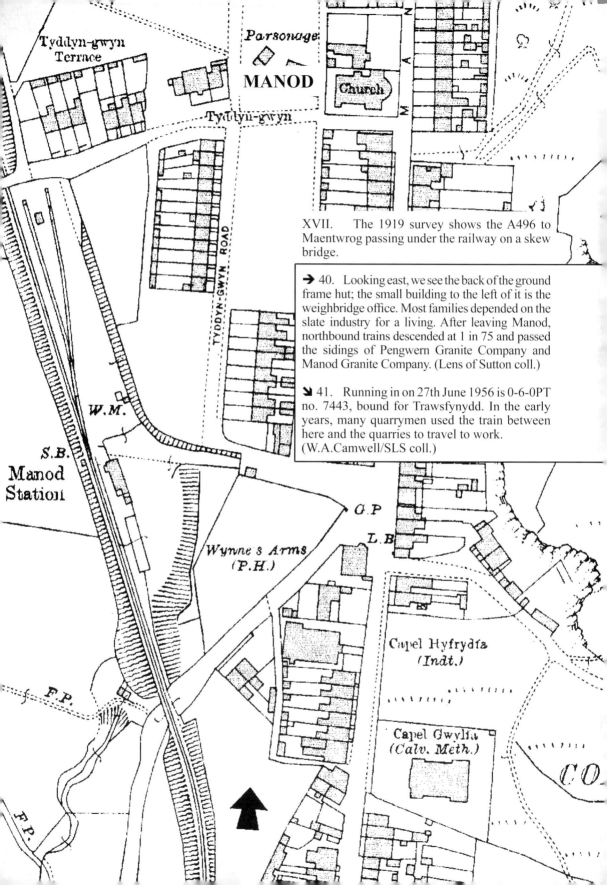

Tyddyn-gwyn
Terrace

Parsonage

MANOD

Church

Tyddyn-gwyn

TYDDYN-GWYN ROAD

W.M.

S.B.
Manod
Station

Wynne's Arms
(P.H.)

F.P.

F.P.

G.P

L.B

Capel Hyfrydfa
(Indt.)

Capel Gwylfa
(Calv. Meth.)

CO

XVII.   The 1919 survey shows the A496 to Maentwrog passing under the railway on a skew bridge.

➜ 40.   Looking east, we see the back of the ground frame hut; the small building to the left of it is the weighbridge office. Most families depended on the slate industry for a living. After leaving Manod, northbound trains descended at 1 in 75 and passed the sidings of Pengwern Granite Company and Manod Granite Company. (Lens of Sutton coll.)

➘ 41.   Running in on 27th June 1956 is 0-6-0PT no. 7443, bound for Trawsfynydd. In the early years, many quarrymen used the train between here and the quarries to travel to work. (W.A.Camwell/SLS coll.)

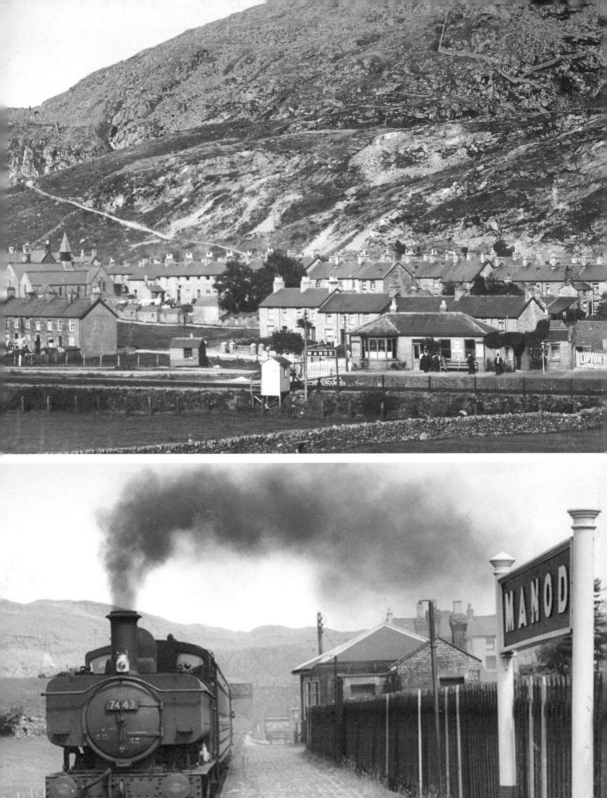

TANYMANOD

42. The location is lower right on the next map, near the waterfalls. The F&BR provided a station and engine shed on the site, which is just behind the camera. One of its two Manning Wardle 0-4-2Ts is seen on the wooden viaduct, which was replaced by a stone one upon gauge conversion. The F&BR conveyed men to the large quarries in Blaenau and also collected slates from the small quarries on its route for transfer to the FR and thence to the ships at Portmadoc. (A.Dudman coll.)

43. There were nine short sidings near the turntable, several of which were used for slate transfer from Craig Ddu Quarry. The engine shed was on No. 5, but only the water tank over it remained in the final years. Part of its support is on the left of the turntable. Whilst turning, it was permitted to leave a wagon on the running line adjacent to the gasworks for coal to be unloaded there. It was in production from 1862 until 1963 and it consumed about 700 tons of coal in the sample years of 1913 and 1947. It is shown on the next map. (K.Robinson coll.)

44.　　The nuclear power station decommissioning plans necessitated a major upgrade to the track, but first a detailed inspection. The arches of Manod Viaduct are being examined on 15th October 1993 by inspectors using a rig under the centre vehicle of this train, which was hauled by no. 31238. (L.Goddard)

45.　　Seen on 9th June 1995 are empty nuclear flasks being a propelled to Trawsfynydd by nos 31134 and 31319. Weighted spacing wagons separate the flask wagons from the brake vans. Empty trains for explosives were also propelled in this manner. (M.J.Stretton)

BLAENAU FFESTINIOG CENTRAL

XVIII. This is the 1920 edition, when the trackwork was at its optimum. The scale is 6ins to 1 mile and the GWR terminus is right of centre and the LMS one left thereof. The former was termed "Central" and the latter "North" from 18th June 1951. The FR from Portmadoc and its first terminus, Dinas (north of the triangle) are on the left. This served passengers until 1870. Its other terminus was at Duffws and its tracks are below Geufron Terrace. There were FR stations close to the standard gauge termini as well; which meant that it had three within ½ mile.

46.	A view east in the 1930s has the GWR platform on the right and on the left is the FR one with its line curving to the terminus at Duffws, just beyond the bridge. FR passenger service ceased on 15th September 1939. Electric lighting was provided on the station from about 1900, DC being generated by the quarries. The staff numbered 14 in 1929, dropping to 10 in 1934. (Lens of Sutton coll.)

47.	Turning round, but 20 years later, we have the end of the GWR route in sight, together with part of the short section of the FR which remained in use long after most of the line closed in 1946. It was leased to the Maenoffen quarry to provide a link between the foot of its incline and the exchange sidings at the LMS station. Its locomotive shed was under the bridge on the left of picture 49. (R.S.Carpenter)

48. The main entrance to the terminal building is on the right of this record of 0-6-0PT no. 7443 with the 11.15am departure for Trawsfynydd on 27th June 1956. Mixed trains were not unusual on the route and they were certainly economical. (W.A.Camwell/SLS coll.)

49. The 2.20pm to Bala waits to leave on 11th August 1956, the FR tracks having become very overgrown. Level ground was at a premium here, hence the curved sidings and provision for engines being made at Tanymanod and carriages at Festiniog. The second "f" in the name was applied from 1951. (B.I.Nathan)

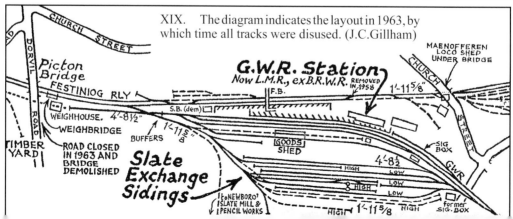

XIX. The diagram indicates the layout in 1963, by which time all tracks were disused. (J.C.Gillham)

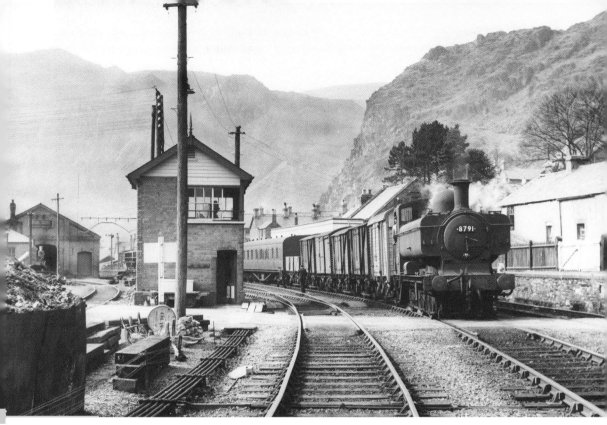

50.   The signal box was opened on 28th September 1926 and replaced two. One was a joint FR/GWR box further west, just beyond the canopy. The FR had become operationally a Light Railway in 1923. The date is 4th April 1959 and the dock is on the right. The goods shed is on the left, with a narrow door for FR stock. The box had 31 levers and closed on 28th January 1961, along with the goods yard. (G.Adams/M.J.Stretton coll.)

51.   We are at the end of the former GWR track in 1959 and the footbridge on the left was the view point for photograph nos 45, 46 and 48. Included is the 6-ton crane. This is the site of the junction of the F&BR with the FR. The last slate was moved over FR rails on 3rd November 1962. The track nearest the left wall had been for slate traffic only, but the adjacent and clearer one was in use until the end. (M.J.Stretton coll.)

BLAENAU FFESTINIOG

52.   The white finish of the Queens Hotel is visible in this view of the same location in February 1982. New track on the right came into use on 20th April 1964 to link the BR branches for the conveyance of nuclear flasks. It was moved to the left and a loop laid in 1981. The new joint BR/FR station is nearing completion in the background, the BR platform coming into use on 22nd March 1982. A tamper is at work, completion having been delayed by snow. (A.G.W.Garraway)

53.   The first FR train arrived at the new station on 25th May 1982, but only its roof can be seen on account of the crowds. The platform had no buildings and only one face at that stage. Tickets were issued in the Tourist Information Centre, which was in a house to the right of this view, for the next 15 years. The new BR platform could take ten coaches. (A.G.W.Garraway)

54.   *Blanche* has just arrived with the 12.20 from Porthmadog on 4th September 1984, by which time temporary buildings had been erected. In the background is the footbridge, which replaced the structure carrying Dorvil Road. Beyond it are two arches; FR trains use the left one, the right one being provided for a possible service to Dinas at the foot of the incline to Llechwedd Quarry. On the right is no. 47565, which is working the 13.30 to Llandudno, its eight coaches spending the remainder of the day on the coast route. The school (left) was built on the site of the GWR goods shed. (T.Heavyside)

55.   No. 47603 stands in the loop line after working the 'Manchester Executive Pullman' on 22nd May 1993. This train had been stabled on Manod Viaduct on the Trawsfynydd line in order to leave the loop clear for the 'Snowdonian' railtour, which had followed the Pullman train along the branch from Llandudno Junction. Double Fairlie 0-4-4-0 *David Lloyd George* waits to depart with a train for Porthmadog. (L.Goddard)

56.   An eastward view from 23rd July 1994 includes the 15.07 to Llandudno Junction and the new buildings for both railways. The Queens Hotel is largely obscured, but it helps to relate this picture with no. 49. The second FR platform has been completed, but it has only a siding at its far end, this being used occasionally for defective stock or a second locomotive. The fine canopy was completed in 1990. "Heritage" DMUs ran until May 2000; a comeback would be widely welcomed, just for the viewing potential. (V.Mitchell)

57.	Two BR Standard Class 4 2-6-4Ts were used on 'The Slate Miner' railtour, which was split at Llandudno Junction with 80079 working the first train to Blaenau Ffestiniog and 80098 following with the second portion. The steep climb to Pont-y-Pant was underestimated with the result that 80079 stalled. No. 80098, left its coaches at Llanrwst North station and pushed the first train to Blaenau Ffestiniog. Both engines returned light for the second train and double-headed it down the branch. Darkness was falling as the two locomotives prepared to work the eight coach train back to Llandudno Junction on 17th October 1999. The second FR loop had been completed, but was not in use. (L.Goddard)

58.	The standard gauge buffer stops are in the distance, as the line to Trawsfynydd was closed in October 1998. It was not lifted. The expensive footbridge became largely redundant and this convenient crossing was soon provided and is seen in September 2009. Part of the Queens Hotel is on the left, some of its lower rooms serving as the FR's shop and ticket office for about ten years. A steel container on the platform formed the vandal proof replacement. (V.Mitchell)

59.   The LNWR provided an impressive terminal building, but it was of timber construction and burnt down in 1951. It is seen on 3rd June 1932, with "Cauliflower" class 2F 0-6-0 no. 8405 waiting to leave at 4.30pm. The sign below the gas lamp even refers to gauge; most unusual. The FR station was across the road. (H.C.Casserley)

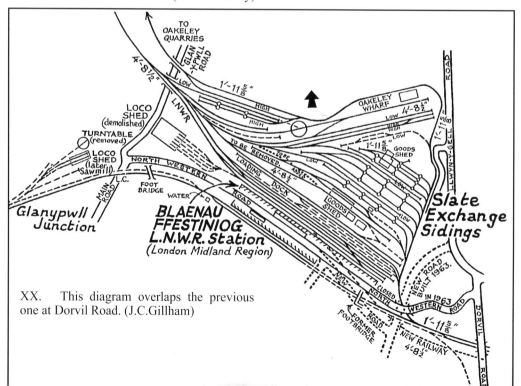

XX.   This diagram overlaps the previous one at Dorvil Road. (J.C.Gillham)

60. Temporary sectional buildings were recorded on 5th August 1954, along with a Morris 10 and 2-6-2T no. 40208. The background is a slate waste tip. (J.W.T.House/C.L.Caddy coll.)

61. More slate waste is evident as we examine the exchange sidings in 1958. The diagram indicates the low standard gauge sidings, which cannot be seen. Two high ones are in the background. (R.S.Carpenter)

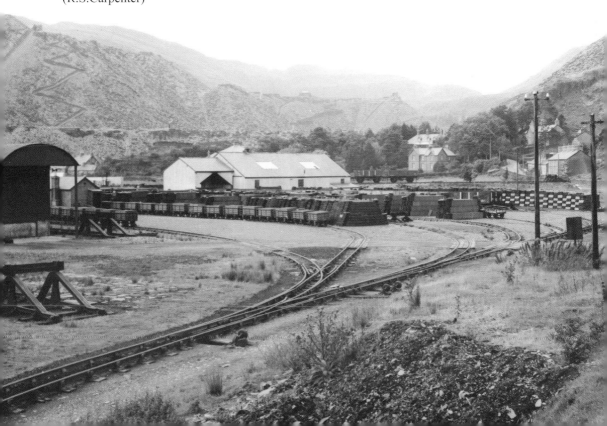

62.   A new station building was completed in 1956 and is seen on 4th April 1959, with a Crosville bus and the North Western Hotel in the background. The latter had been sold by the LNWR in 1906. The suffix "North" was used from 18th June 1951 until 6th May 1968. On the left is one of two goods sheds. General freight ceased on 4th May 1964, but wagon load traffic continued until 1982. (G.Adams/M.J.Stretton coll.)

63.   A remarkable out-of-gauge load arrived on 19th February 1961 in the form of a 123-ton transformer for the Tanygrisiau Power Station. Its lower lake had severed the FR, but one of its water tanks remained standing in the background. Less than one inch clearance was reported in the tunnel. The train was hauled by EE Type 1 no. D8036, which came specially from London and was the first diesel locomotive on the branch. At the rear was a class 4F 0-6-0. The 18-lever signal box was in use from 10th March 1931 to 25th September 1966. Its predecessor had a 30-lever frame. (British Railways)

64.   Shunting on 16th July 1964 is 2-6-2T no. 41244 and on the left is a new bus garage, which was built on the site of the old carriage shed. It was unusually combined with an engine shed and closed on 14th September 1931. On the right is the weighbridge and its office. (C.L.Caddy)

65.   A photograph from 12th July 1965 shows the signal controlling the line to Trawsfynydd and that the platform had to be curved to accommodate the new alignment. The diagram shows the new roads and in the distance are two new bridge spans. The left one was for the line seen on the left of picture 58, but traffic ceased before it could be used. (C.L.Caddy)

66.   The last flask train is seen entering Blaenau Ffestiniog on 22nd April 1997, behind no. 37426, one of the very few instances of class 37 haulage on this train. This was an additional flask train sent to load a single rod, which was found during the decommissioning process! The train returned, with 31 haulage, a week later. The class 37 is on the first part of the new link and the closed station is behind the train. (K.Robinson)

For other views, refer to Middleton Press albums:
Branch Lines around Portmadoc 1923-46
Branch Lines around Porthmadog 1954-94
Festiniog - 50 years of Enterprise
Festiniog in the Fifties
Festiniog in the Sixties
Return to Blaenau 1970-82

67.   The main line from the terminus is in the lower left corner and the Oakeley Quarry sidings are above it. Llechwedd Quarry's sidings and crane are lower centre in the postcard view. The FR's Dinas terminus was to the left, but all its tracks in this area were lifted in 1950. Llechwedd Quarry made a new connection between its wharf and incline. (Lens of Sutton coll.)

68. The building houses the Pant-yr-Afon power station of Llechwedd Quarry. Its 1905 generators were still in use in 2005 and some of its DC went through rotary convertors into the local mains from 1931. Some of the heavy rainfall had already gone through the Maenofferen Quarry generators. A new environmental tax on primary aggregates prompted research to be carried out to evaluate the practical potential for the use of slate waste as secondary aggregates. The Conwy Valley line appeared to be the most sustainable for waste from Oakeley and Llechwedd quarries and so trials involving load and braking tests were carried out on the 1-in-90 climb to Ffestiniog Tunnel. No. 66514 is pictured leaving the tunnel with twenty JNA wagons on 17th November 2002. The bore is 2 miles 206yds in length. (L.Goddard)

69.   Virgin 'Voyager' No. 220017 *Bombardier Voyager* was being gauge-tested between Llandudno Junction and Blaenau Ffestiniog on 17th March 2003. The unit is seen passing the site of the Festiniog Railway's original Dinas terminus as well as its new carriage shed. Trains have to reverse to access it. (L.Goddard)

ROMAN BRIDGE

70. A view down the Lledr Valley in 1957 features the facilities for ladies, which were separate from the main building. However, staffing ceased on 6th August 1956 and freight service was withdrawn then. (J.H.Moss/R.S.Carpenter coll.)

April 1943

LLANDUDNO JUNCTION, BETTWS-Y-COED, and BLAENAU FESTINIOG.

Miles	Down.	Week Days only. mrn		mrn	mrn S	mrn E		non E	aft S	aft		aft	aft	
—	Llandudno Junc....dep.	5 25	..	8 5	1043	1110	..	12 6	1223	3 0	..	6 9	8 15	..
1½	Glan Conway...........	..	..	8 9	1047	1114	..	12 4	1227	3 4	..	6 4	..	..
5	Tal-y-Cafn G...........	5 36	..	8 20	1054	1122	..	1214	1235	3 10	..	6 12	8 27	..
8	Dolgarrog	5 43	..	8 32	11 1	1129	..	1223	1242	3 18	..	6 19	8 35	..
11¼	Llanrwst and Trefriw	5 54	..	8 40	11 9	1138	..	1232	1250	3 26	..	6 28	8 47	..
15	Bettws-y-Coed P arr.	6 3	..	8 49	1117	1146	..	1240	1259	3 34	..	6 37	8 59	..
	dep.	6 6	..	8 55	1125	1154	..	..	1 10	3 37	..	6 43	9 8	..
19¾	Pont-y-pant	..	..	9 7	1137	12 6	..	..	1 22	3 49	..	6 55	9 15	..
20¾	Dolwyddelen............	6 22	..	9 13	1144	1213	..	..	1 29	3 56	..	7 1	9 21	..
22¼	Roman Bridge	6 29	..	9 20	1150	1219	..	..	1 36	4 4	..	7 10	9 29	..
27¼	BlaenauFestiniog W arr.	6 41	..	9 33	12 3	1232	..	..	1 48	4 16	..	7 22	9 41	..

Miles	Up	Week Days only. mrn	mrn S	mrn E		aft S	aft E	aft S	aft E	aft	aft	aft E	aft S
—	Blaenau Festiniog..dep.	7 20	1020	1110	..	1225	..	2 5	2 55	4 30	8 5	10 5	10 5
4½	Roman Bridge............	7 30	1030	1120	..	1236	..	2 16	3 6	4 41	8 16	1015	1015
6½	Dolwyddelen............	7 37	1037	1126	..	1241	..	2 21	3 12	4 46	8 22	1020	1020
8	Pont-y-pant.............	7 40	1040	1130	..	1245	..	2 25	3 17	4 50	8 26	..	..
12¼	Bettws-y-Coed P.. arr.	7 52	1051	1141	..	1256	..	2 36	3 28	5 11	8 37	1034	1034
	dep.	7 54	1054	1150	..	1 0	1 0	2 40	3 36	5 14	8 40	..	1037
16	Llanrwst and Trefriw....	8 5	11 5	1158	..	1 8	1 8	2 47	3 43	5 22	8 48	..	1044
19½	Dolgarrog...............	8 12	1118	12 5	..	1 15	1 15	2 54	3 50	5 29	8 55	..	.
22¼	Tal-y-Cafn G............	8 22	1127	1214	..	1 23	1 23	3 5	3 58	5 37	9 5	..	1058
26	Glan Conway ....(510	8 29	1134	1221	..	1 30	1 30	3 12	4 5	5 44	..	..	..
27½	Llandudno Jnc. 506, arr.	8 34	1139	1226	..	1 35	1 35	3 24	4 10	5 49	9 15	..	1116

E Except Sats. **G** Tal-y-Cafn & Eglwysbach. **P** Sta. for Capel Curig. **S** Sats. only **W** Blaenau Festiniog ¼ mile to G.W. Sta.

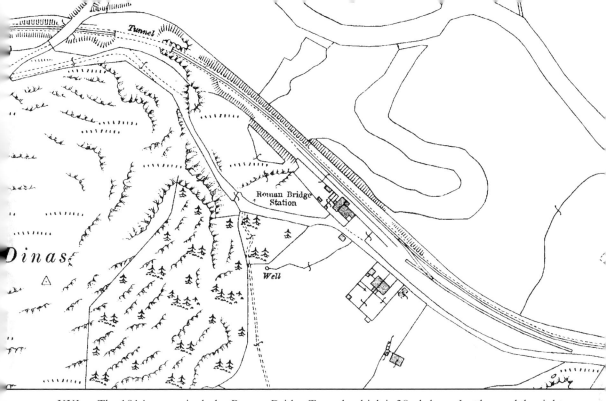

XXI.   The 1914 survey includes Roman Bridge Tunnel, which is 38yds long. Just beyond the right border is Bertheos Tunnel, 46yds in length.

71.   A 1965 record includes the two oil lamps, plus the arrangements for gentlemen. The building was little changed in 2010, but a modern waiting shelter had been added. The summit of Snowdon can be seen on a clear day. (C.L.Caddy)

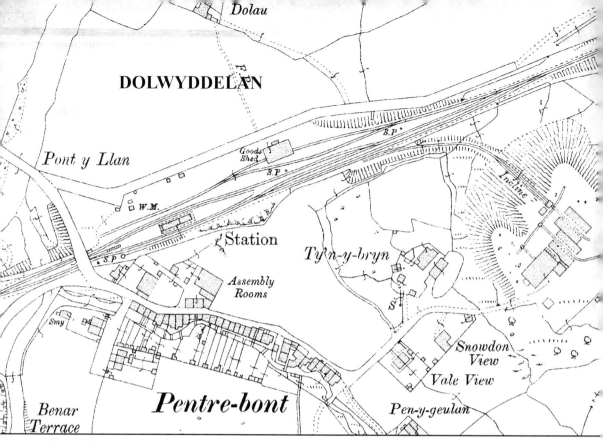

XXII. The name was mis-spelt Dolwyddel**e**n by the railways from 1880 until 1980. The slate quarries of the valley suffered poor transport until the coming of the railway and then they did not have the advantage of economy of scale nor of top quality material. Tyn-y-bryn Quarry (right) opened in the 1860s and had four levels. It was the only one in the Lledr and Conwy Valleys to have a siding and it closed in 1924.

72.   A panorama from around 1930 features the island platform and footbridge to it, which were unique on the branch. The building on the right with two courses of light brick is the weighbridge office. (Lens of Sutton coll.)

73. The water tank supply was used by almost all down trains owing to the stiff climb in the Lledr Valley. The catch points were to deal with any runaways on the incline. (D.K.Jones coll.)

74. The goods yard closed on 4th May 1964, it having lost the spacious goods shed shown on the map, about six years earlier. It had a 30cwt crane and was replaced by the hut on the left. The white shelter on the platform was added in September 1956 to protect the 15 signal levers and the instruments. They were not used after staffing ceased on 5th June 1966 and neither were the tracks to the left of the platform. It seems that Brunel's Chalet design was copied, but did not include the ornate ventilator for the toilets. (Lens of Sutton coll.)

75.   No. 153327 waits for the photographer on 6th September 2009, as the sole remaining platform was recorded. Direct level access to it was at last possible, using the gateway on the left and the site of the goods yard. Invisible is the fibre optic cable recently laid along the branch. It was extended alongside the FR to the Cambrian Coast to create a secure ring main for Network Rail. Even more extensive floral displays were added in 2010. The Conwy Valley Community Rail Partnership is the oldest such organisation in Wales and ensures that the stations are well maintained. We must all be grateful and wish that they could restore end windows on trains for vista appreciation. Roman Bridge and here will both take four coaches. (V.Mitchell)

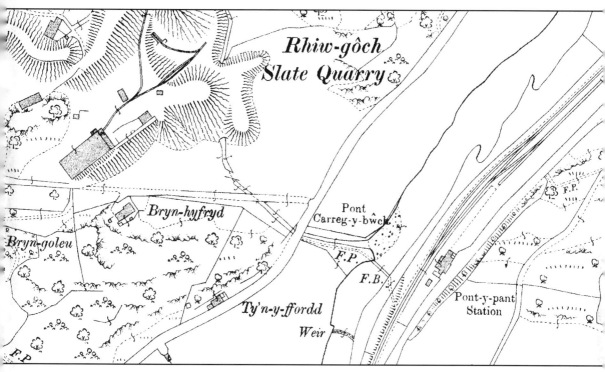

XXIII. The 1913 survey includes a quarry, which had probably just closed. It was formed of a large deep pit which was started in the 1860s, with a few adits off it. The loop was lost in about 1951 and the siding closed to goods traffic on 6th May 1964.

76. There was a signal box containing a ground frame, opposite the main station building in the 1920s and later. A train is approaching Pont-y-Pant Upper Tunnel (66yds) in the background; Lower (144yds) is behind us. The platform takes five coaches. East of the station is the 117yd long Beaverpool Tunnel. (HMRS)

77.   It is 3rd June 1932 and we are looking back from a down train at the observation car. Beyond the platform end was a sign demanding that all goods trains must have their brakes pinned down. The station became unstaffed on 23rd June 1966. (H.C.Casserley)

78.   The provisions were similar to those made at Roman Bridge and are seen in better lighting in about 1960. Both became private residences and have been well cared for. (J.H.Moss/R.S.Carpenter coll.)

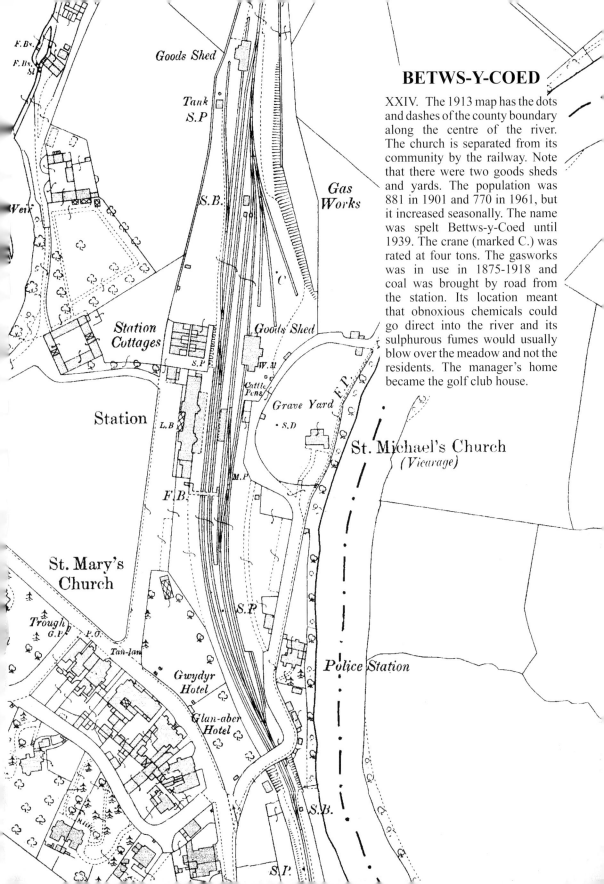

BETWS-Y-COED

XXIV. The 1913 map has the dots and dashes of the county boundary along the centre of the river. The church is separated from its community by the railway. Note that there were two goods sheds and yards. The population was 881 in 1901 and 770 in 1961, but it increased seasonally. The name was spelt Bettws-y-Coed until 1939. The crane (marked C.) was rated at four tons. The gasworks was in use in 1875-1918 and coal was brought by road from the station. Its location meant that obnoxious chemicals could go direct into the river and its sulphurous fumes would usually blow over the meadow and not the residents. The manager's home became the golf club house.

Goods Shed

Tank
S.P

S.B.

Gas
Works

Station
Cottages

S.P

Goods Shed

W.M

Cattle
Pens

Grave Yard

· S.D

St. Michael's Church
(Vicarage)

Station

L.B

Weir

F.Bs.

F.Bs.
St

M.P

F.B.

St. Mary's
Church

Trough
G.P.

P.O

Tan-lan

Gwydyr
Hotel

Glan-aber
Hotel

S.P.

Police Station

S.B.

S.P.

79.   Departing north in 1955 is an ex-LMS 2-6-2T and it is coupled to one of the popular observation cars. One is still running on the Bluebell Railway. The platform on the left came into use in July 1898, along with a covered footbridge. (J.H.Moss/R.S.Carpenter coll.)

80.   The 30-lever No. 1 signal box is in the distance and opposite it had been the engine shed of the terminus. It had become a goods shed and was partially demolished in the 1930s. The second signal box is shown on the map, south of the station; it had an 18-lever frame. Both boxes closed on 5th June 1966. (D.K.Jones coll.)

81.   A northward view from the 1960s includes a camping coach at the former slate wharf and the end of the goods shed. Freight traffic ceased on 4th May 1964. Termed the "Gateway to Snowdonia", the town has an open-top bus service in the Summer to the foot of Snowdon. Sadly it does not continue to Caernarfon, making a circular tour, via Porthmadog, difficult. (Dr G.B.Sutton)

82.   The station master had the upper floor as his dwelling, plus the lower left part. This view is from June 1967; regular staffing had ceased 12 months earlier, but the building continues to be busy, mainly for gastronomic reasons. (C.L.Caddy)

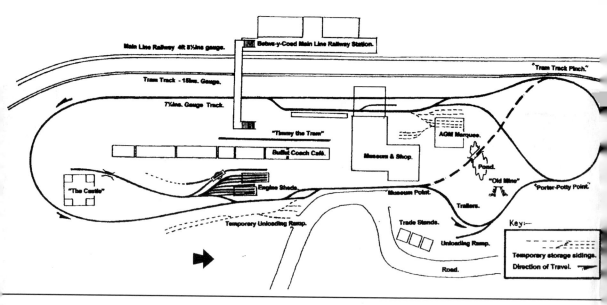

The diagram shows a layout of the Conway Valley Railway Museum including the following labelled features: "Main Line Railway 4ft 8½ins gauge.", "Betws-y-Coed Main Line Railway Station.", "Tram Track - 15ins. Gauge.", "7¼ins. Gauge Track.", "Timmy the Tram", "Buffet Coach Café.", "Museum & Shop.", "AGM Marquee.", "Tram Track Pinch.", "Road.", "The Castle", "Engine Sheds.", "Museum Point.", "Old Mine", "Porter-Potty Point.", "Trailers.", "Temporary Unloading Ramp.", "Trade Stands.", "Unloading Ramp.", "Road.", "Key:—", "Temporary storage sidings.", "Direction of Travel."

XXV.   The Conway Valley Railway Museum was developed in the 1970s by Alan Pratt, much of the 7¼ ins gauge track having point rodding laid on its side as rail. The enterprise was acquired in 1985 by Colin Cartwright and the track was eventually more than doubled in length. This is the layout in 2006, by which time a whole day was needed to fully enjoy the extensive displays. The telephone number is 01690 710132.

83.   The 16.40 from Blaenau Ffestiniog stands at the 5-car platform near the new canopy on the restaurant on 2nd August 1992. The North Wales Railway Circle provided the circular board. In the distance is the 110 volt overhead wire and its tramcar. The diagram shows that its track was subsequently extended close to the main line and under the footbridge, from which we are looking. It replaced the line near the fence. (P.G.Barnes)

84.   This 3-car platform was opened on 29th July 1989 and as it was close to the town centre "North" was added to the name of the original station. The 15.03 from Blaenau Ffestiniog is calling on 6th September 2009 and is about to run through the 85yd long Llanrwst Tunnel. The 153 units were to be fitted with higher seats in 2011, to improve the view. (V.Mitchell)

London & North Western Ry
Issued subject to the conditions &regulations in the Cos Time Tables Books Bills & Notices.
TAL-Y-CAFN & EGLWYS BACH TO
BLAENAU FESTINIOG (LNW)
Third] 408(S) [Class
BLAENAU FESTINIOG
TURN OVER) FARE 1/10
JL 9009 9426

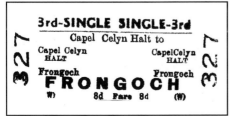

3rd-SINGLE SINGLE-3rd
Capel Celyn Halt to
Capel Celyn HALT   CapelCelyn HALT
Frongoch   Frongoch
FRONGOCH
W)   8d Fare 8d   (W)
327   327

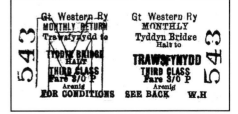

Gt Western Ry   Gt Western Ry
MONTHLY RETURN   MONTHLY
Trawsfynydd to   Tyddyn Bridge
                       Halt to
TYDDYN BRIDGE   **TRAWSFYNYDD**
HALT
THIRD CLASS   THIRD CLASS
Fare 3/0 P   Fare 3/0 P
Arenig   Arenig
FOR CONDITIONS   SEE BACK   W.H
543   543

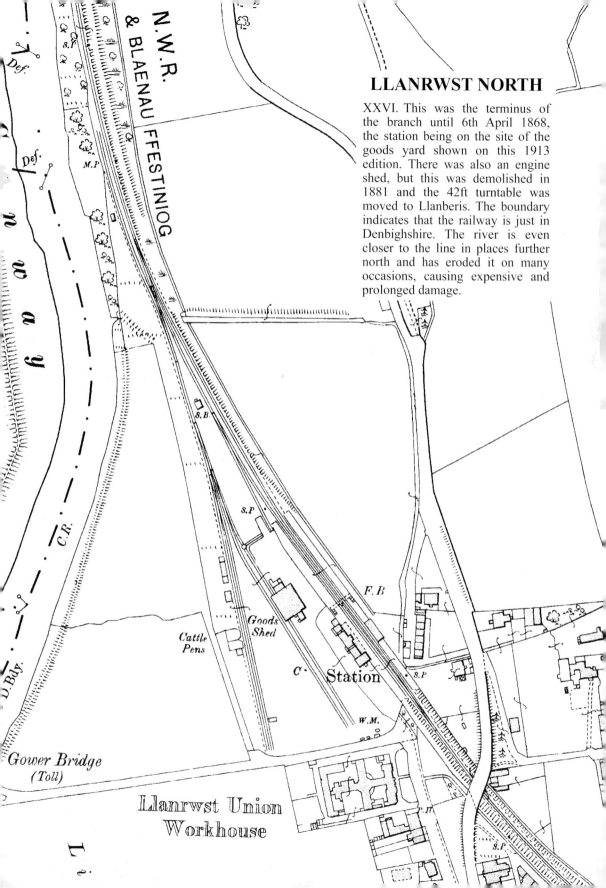

LLANRWST NORTH

XXVI. This was the terminus of the branch until 6th April 1868, the station being on the site of the goods yard shown on this 1913 edition. There was also an engine shed, but this was demolished in 1881 and the 42ft turntable was moved to Llanberis. The boundary indicates that the railway is just in Denbighshire. The river is even closer to the line in places further north and has eroded it on many occasions, causing expensive and prolonged damage.

85.   A view north in about 1960 shows the full name. Between here and Dolgarrog there was Abbey Siding and Tanlan Siding during the 1930s, at least. (Lens of Sutton coll.)

86.   We now have two photographs from the 1950s. This is a southward view from the footbridge. The population was then around 2500. Annual goods inward in that period included 2000 tons of bagged fertiliser and 1500 tons of feedstuffs. Outward was 1000 tons of zinc ore. (R.S.Carpenter)

87.	The goods shed was more than that; it was used to store bagged fertiliser and seed for distribution. The bogie van on stilts increased space further. On the left is the 10-ton crane. A 2-6-2T was derailed

88.	Station staffing ended on 23rd May 1966 and the building was subsequently let. This is its condition in May 1988, complete with portable steps. The name was "Llanrwst & Trefriw" from April 1884 until 6th May 1974, when the suffix was dropped. "North" was added in July 1989. (A.C.Mott)

on the points at the south end of the loop by a kitten on 29th October 1958. It was trapped by the blade. Freight service was withdrawn on 2nd December 1968. (J.H.Moss/R.S.Carpenter coll.)

89.   Portable steps also appear in this view. This one is from 6th September 2009 and includes the signal box, which had a 20-lever frame. It controlled the only intermediate loop on the branch and drivers had to creep past it to handle the tokens. Both platforms take six coaches. (V.Mitchell)

DOLGARROG

XXVII. The 1948 survey has the station on the right with the private line to Dolgarrog Aluminium Works taking a U-shape course west from it. Production started in 1908 and water transport was used initially, the wharf being near the northern corner of the premises. A 40-ton steam boat called *Pioneer* was used and the canal was completed in 1914, with a 2ft gauge railway within the works.

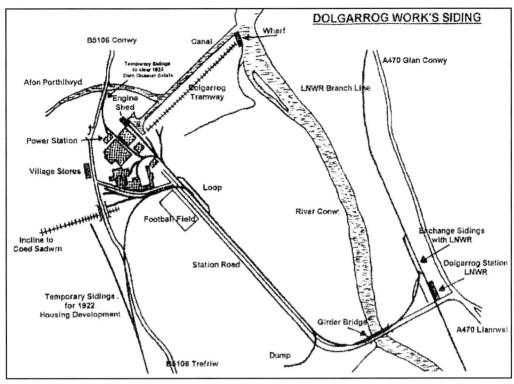

XXVIII. The diagram shows the Aluminium Corporation's system at its optimum, in the early 1920s. The incline on the left was of 2ft gauge and linked with a line which ran west across the hills from about 1906, in connection with the construction of the Eigiau and Coedty dams. These powered electrical generators, both AC and DC. Sadly, both dams failed at 9.15pm on 2nd November 1925 and 16 residents died, while others were enjoying films in the village hall. The furnaces in the works exploded randomly and all lighting ceased, adding to the terror. The line from the LNWR was completed in 1916, by which time the ore came from Norway. It required enormous electrical energy for its smelting and processing. By 1928, the LMS Works at Crewe was receiving energy from here and also Maentwrog. Two more dams followed and the long line in the hills lasted until 1984.

90.　　There were two 0-6-0STs and ten wagons initially. One of the engines was Hunslet no. 761 of 1902, called *Uxbridge*, as it had worked on the construction of the line between there and Harrow. It is seen near the football field in the 1940s. Two coaches were purchased for the conveyance of workers and these were used until 1932. (A.Pratt/Dolgarrog Rly. Soc.)

91.   Another 1940s view and this is towards the works, which was producing around four tons of aluminium per week during World War I and 100 by the end of WWII, when smelting ceased. However, new generators came in the 1950s and rolling continued, with ingots arwriving by rail, but this was discontinued in about 1962. The rails went to the new Welsh Highland Railway in 1963. (A.Pratt/Dolgarrog Rly. Soc.)

92.   The tiny station opened on 18th December 1916 and was electrically lit. We view the platform and level crossing in the early 1960s, with the loop behind us. The station closed on 26th October 1964, but reopened on 14th June 1965, after protests. A footpath has been established on the former railway bridge across the river, but the stop remains equally stark and devoid of buildings. It takes only two coaches. (Lens of Sutton coll.)

93.   The Dolgarrog Railway Society started to restore the line and stock on site in August 2010 included *Taurus*, a 1951 Drewry, Vulcan Works no. D139. It had worked at Erith and Salford. (Dolgarrog Railway Society)

TAL-Y-CAFN

94.   The station is the nearest to the famous National Trust Bodnant Gardens. There was no signal box, but there was a 15-lever frame on the platform, to the left of the "Coal Tank", no. 7796. On the right of this 1942 photograph is a short platform, which was adjacent to the goods shed. The remaining platform takes five coaches. (A.W.V.Mace/Milepost 92½)

Landing Stage

C. C. at L. (Disused)

Tal-y-cafn Bridge (Toll)

Pen-rhiw

W.

Tal-y-cafn Terrace

Oil Tank

Tal-y-cafn Farm

on & R.D.Bdy.

Toll House

H.W.M.O.T

Ty'n-y-borth

S.P

Tal-y-cafn Hotel

Station

W.M.

Post Office

Tal-y-cafn

Liable to Floods

Auction Mart

Cattle Pen

S.P

.C

XXIX. The 1913 survey reveals another station in Denbighshire and a rare direct connection between the cattle dock and the market. The river had been forded here in Roman times. The suffix "& Eglwysbach" was applied from 1888 to 1974.

Meddiant Cottage

95.   Leaving Tal-y-Cafn for Blaenau Festiniog in April 1942 is no. 28337. The leading wagon was provided for the timber to overhang. The goods yard closed on 4th May 1964. (A.W.V.Mace/Milepost 92½)

96.   Seen on the same day is "Precursor" class 4-4-0 no. 25277 shunting the Cattle Fair special, but its cattle wagons obscure the cattle dock, not to mention the cattle. (A.W.V.Mace/Milepost 92½)

97.   The 1940s frame had 15 levers and was behind the wall on the left of picture 94. An oil lamp is on the right and the instruments are in the box at the back. (L.Davies coll.)

98.   The loop was last used on 24th September 1966 and the frame was later reduced to five levers. It was moved to the hut on the left and was out of use by 1982, but the gates were still worked by hand, with fixed distant signals on each approach. The Dolgarrog Railway Society had much of its rolling stock stored here from about 1995 to 2004. (D.K.Jones coll.)

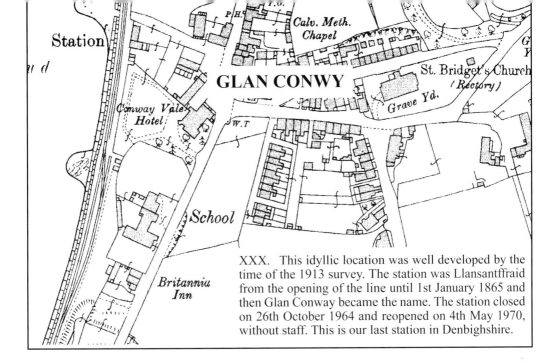

GLAN CONWY

XXX. This idyllic location was well developed by the time of the 1913 survey. The station was Llansantffraid from the opening of the line until 1st January 1865 and then Glan Conway became the name. The station closed on 26th October 1964 and reopened on 4th May 1970, without staff. This is our last station in Denbighshire.

99.   Seen in the early 1960s, the platform has a pathway under it to the beach and a parcels shed on the left. In the distance is a camping coach with a fine view. There was also one here in the 1930s, but there were no more after the goods yard closed on 4th May 1964.
(Lens of Sutton coll.)

100.   A northward view in July 1966 has a porch and weeds en-croaching on the plat-form. However, condi-tions improved after the reopening and the name was changed to Glan Conwy in 1980. Part of the platform was raised in 2000. The Royal Train had stopped here overnight in 1953 - the views are superb. The platform takes five coaches. (C.L.Caddy)

EAST OF
LLANDUDNO JUNCTION

101. The station is in the background and the mailbag catcher is on the right as a 2-6-2T crosses to the Blaenau branch in June 1947. The connection was moved further east later. Partially obscured by the signals on the left is No. 1 Box, which had 101 levers and was open from 31st October 1897 until 26th May 1968. (M.Whitehouse coll.)

→ 102. An unusual 5-car DMU formation has left platform 1 at 10.35 on 7th August 1983 working the "Sunday Shuttle" to Blaenau Ffestiniog for Gwynedd County Council. In the foreground is the Up Passenger Loop, which joins the Up Main behind the camera. (D.H.Mitchell)

→ 103. The "Conway Climber" railtour on 11th April 1999 originated at Milton Keynes and class 4 4-6-0 no. 45407 is about to bear right onto the Conwy Valley Line. The parallel curve leads to Heron Fuels oil depot and the two nearer sidings serve Glan Conwy freight depot. Access to these is via the line on the left of picture 102. (P.G.Barnes)

LLANDUDNO JUNCTION

XXXI. The main line is across this 1913 map and the branch to Llandudno is top left. The early station had five platforms, two on the branch, one up plus two down. They were thus very short and inconvenient. Conway Valley trains used the single line along the waterfront

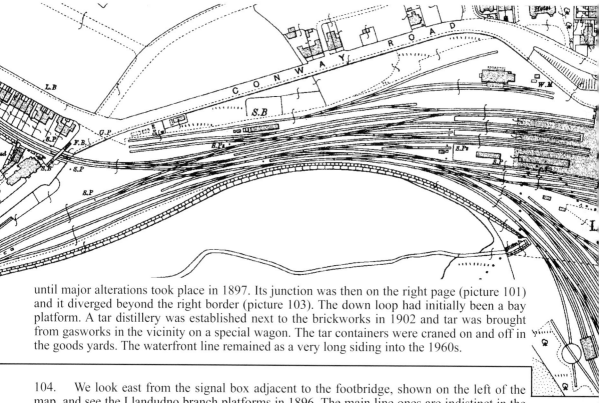

until major alterations took place in 1897. Its junction was then on the right page (picture 101) and it diverged beyond the right border (picture 103). The down loop had initially been a bay platform. A tar distillery was established next to the brickworks in 1902 and tar was brought from gasworks in the vicinity on a special wagon. The tar containers were craned on and off in the goods yards. The waterfront line remained as a very long siding into the 1960s.

104.   We look east from the signal box adjacent to the footbridge, shown on the left of the map, and see the Llandudno branch platforms in 1896. The main line ones are indistinct in the background. The road was numbered A55 in 1919. The new station was built a little to the east and then this site was cleared. (British Railways)

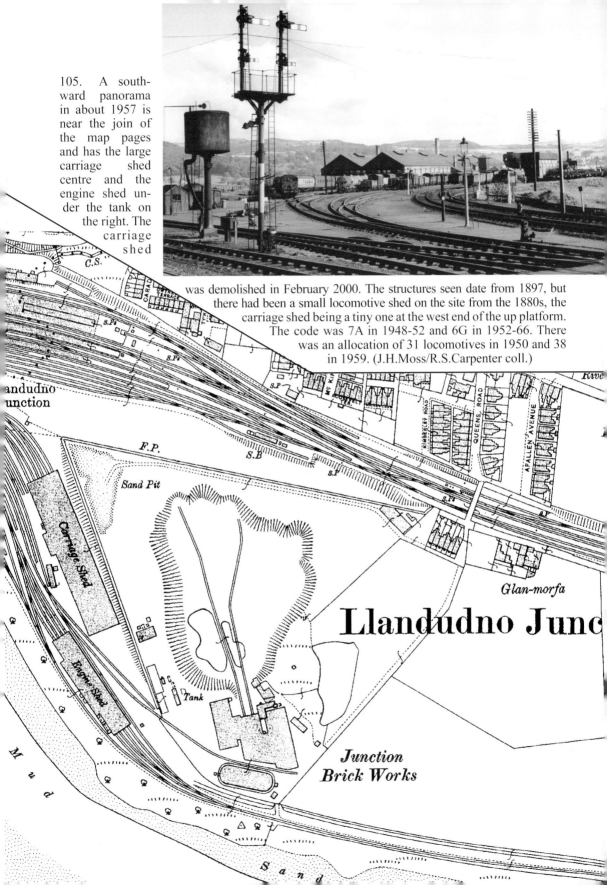

105. A south-ward panorama in about 1957 is near the join of the map pages and has the large carriage shed centre and the engine shed under the tank on the right. The carriage shed was demolished in February 2000. The structures seen date from 1897, but there had been a small locomotive shed on the site from the 1880s, the carriage shed being a tiny one at the west end of the up platform. The code was 7A in 1948-52 and 6G in 1952-66. There was an allocation of 31 locomotives in 1950 and 38 in 1959. (J.H.Moss/R.S.Carpenter coll.)

106.   The 1897 station was spacious and well designed; it still serves travellers well, particularly the buffet. Two dated signs are evident as a DMU for Blaenau Ffestiniog waits in about 1957. The further one states TELEGRAPH OFFICE. Gas lighting prevails. (J.H.Moss/R.S.Carpenter coll.)

107.   Lifts were provided in line with all three flights of steps, but the main entrance was not impressive. The span on the right passes over the track at platform 1. In recent years, the platform capacities have been: No. 1-15, No. 2 (west bay) - 5, No. 3-15 and No. 4-11 coaches. (D.A.Thompson)

108.   The 18.05 to Llandudno departs on 6th August 1985 and we have the opportunity to see the new signal box, which opened with a panel on 9th February 1985, plus the old 154-lever frame box of 1889. This closed that day and it had been No. 2 until May 1968. (D.H.Mitchell)

109.   No. 31420 is running in with the 17.40 Llandudno to Manchester train on 21st August 1990. The bridge for the A547 is on the site of the level crossing, the A55 having been put in immersed tubes at the bottom of the River Conwy. Tunnelling was not possible, but it does pass under the main lines on the left of this picture. (T.Heavyside)

DEGANWY

XXXII. The 1912 map at 20 ins to 1 mile features the slate loading pier completed by the LNWR when it reached Blaenau's quarries. The complex of narrow gauge tracks were for small wagons, which were loaded in batches of four on special transporter wagons and unloaded here. The system was a failure for several commercial reasons, notably that most of the slate shipped from Portmadoc was destined for places south thereof. Thus the LNWR could not compete for that business. Note that many inland plots carry spacious houses. The pier sidings were used mainly for carriage storage.

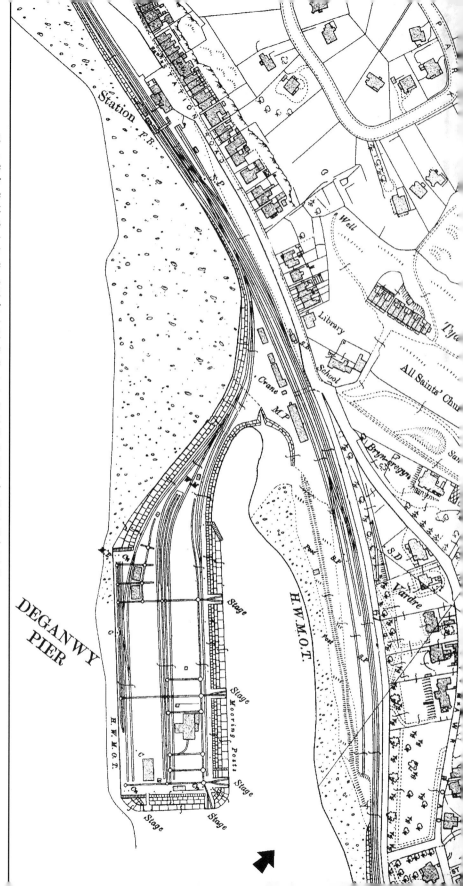

110.   This southward view is from the footbridge featured in picture 113 and is from about 1912. The connection to the local goods yard is included. The station did not open until 1st May 1866. (Lens of Sutton coll.)

111.   Passing through on 6th August 1955 is 4-6-0 no. 46168 *The Girl Guide*, a "Royal Scot" class locomotive. Near the rear coach is No. 1 Box, which had 26 levers and was in use from March 1884 until May 1967. (J.W.T.House/C.L.Caddy coll.)

112.   Since photograph 110 was taken, the station had received a fully glazed parcels shed and a new canopy, with stanchions. In the distance in this 1960 picture is the goods yard, which closed on 7th September 1964. It had a 5-ton crane. (R.M.Casserley)

113.   No. 47281 creeps in with the 15.20 Llandudno to Sheffield on 23rd August 1975. Staffing of the station ceased on 2nd May 1977, but the 1914 18-lever signal box in the background was still in use in 2010. The station building was demolished in about 1996, but both platforms still took nine coaches in 2010. (T.Heavyside)

LLANDUDNO

XXXIII. The first station had two platforms until 1892. This extract is from the 1912 edition and has the private siding to the gasworks inset. Three tracks continued south to No. 1 Box until it closed on 13th September 1970. It had 15 levers and controlled access to the carriage sidings on the left. Their length totalled almost two miles, including those east of the running lines. The goods yard (top right) could take 98 wagons. The gasworks was in production from 1854 until 1956, when the grid arrived. In a sample year (1912) 7700 tons of coal and 300 tons of cannel coal arrived by rail. The latter was an oil-rich coal, which generated a yellow flame.

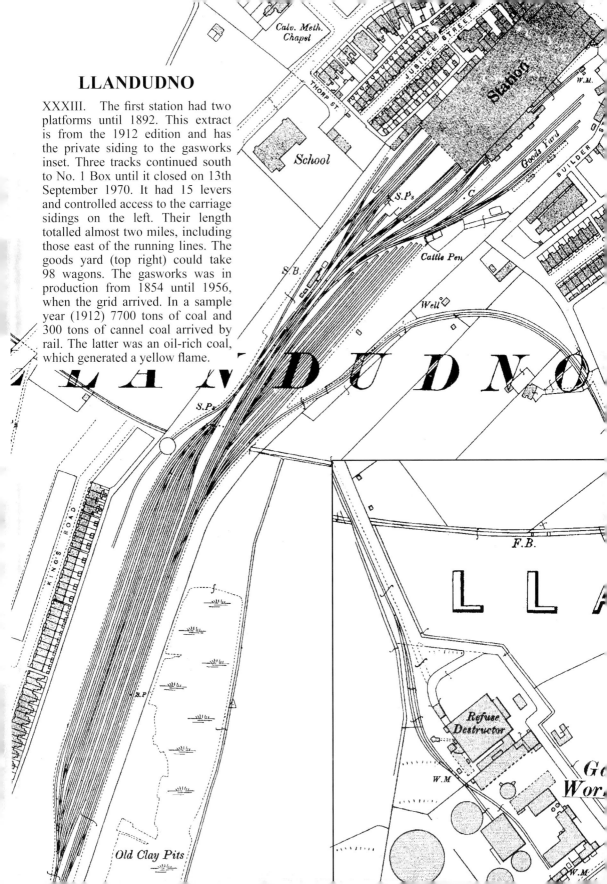

114.	This facade was started in 1892. Platforms 1 and 2 are on the left of the cab road and 3 to 5 are to the right of it. The station was deemed complete in 1903. (British Railways)

115.	The 4.5pm to Birmingham was headed by 4-6-0 no. 45417 on 4th August 1963, when the roof was still complete and with its screens in place. On the right can be seen the jib of the 5-ton crane; the goods yard closed on 3rd April 1967, but continued as a coal depot until 31st May 1976. (R.M.Casserley)

116.   The 1892 signal box had an 86-lever frame and was termed No. 2 until 1970. It was still in use 40 years later, when there were only three down sidings and one up remaining. (J.H.Moss/R.S.Carpenter coll.)

Issued by the L. & N. W. R. Co., subject to the Company's regulations, and to the conditions in their Time Tables.

Llandudno To   H:W.

Conway

Third/ 406 CONWAY \Class   2653

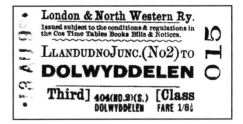

London & North Western Ry.

Issued subject to the conditions & regulations in the Cos Time Tables Books Bills & Notices.

LlandudnoJunc.(No2) To

DOLWYDDELEN

Third] 404(No.2)(S.) [Class 015
         DOLWYDDELEN FARE 1/8½

117.   The deserted cab road was recorded on 15th July 1973, with the 18.58 return excursion to Plymouth (left) and the 19.28 to Liverpool (right). The wall on the left marks the original extent of the roof. (D.H.Mitchell coll.)

118.   With only two axles per car, "Pacer" no. 142056 leaves at 14.11 for Llandudno Junction on 13th May 1988, while class 150 "Sprinter" units wait to work main line services. Both classes were tried on the Conwy Valley line in 1986-87, but were soon banned, the biggest problem being severe wheel squeal. (T.Heavyside)

119.　　Further reduction of the roof had taken place and only platforms 1 to 3 were in use. No. 175009 is bound for Manchester on 6th September 2009; all the platforms could still take ten coaches. There were sidings at platforms 4 and 5 for storage only. (V.Mitchell)

120.　　The sad exterior was recorded from an open-top bus on the same day, by which time only the ticket office was staffed. Regular through trains from London ceased for about 40 years, but were reinstated on 27th September 2004, only to be withdrawn again on 12th December 2008. Work was to start in 2011 on a transport interchange on the site of platforms 4 and 5, plus the surrounding area. (V.Mitchell)

MP Middleton Press

EVOLVING THE ULTIMATE RAIL ENCYCLOPEDIA

Easebourne Lane, Midhurst, West Sussex.
GU29 9AZ Tel:01730 813169

www.middletonpress.co.uk   email:info@middletonpress.co.uk
A-978 0 906520 B- 978 1 873793 C- 978 1 901706 D-978 1 904474 E- 978 1 906008

All titles listed below were in print at time of publication - please check current availability by looking at our website - *www.middletonpress.co.uk* or by requesting a Brochure which includes our *LATEST* RAILWAY TITLES also our TRAMWAY, TROLLEYBUS, MILITARY and WATERWAYS series

96